What they

Defeating the 8 L_____ __ _____

by Geraldine Markel, Ph.D.

"Readers of this book are in for a real treat! Books that address the issues of increasing one's productivity *generally* fall into one of 2 categories. Some are drab, clinical descriptions that drone on about the physiology of brain function and dysfunction. The very person needing the information may not be capable of plodding through the endless detail. Or, some are "cute" and metaphoric, but without practical strategies to accompany the gimmick! This book combines the format of both categories. It entertains the reader while arming him with an arsenal of practical choices to adapt to one's real life. As a career counselor, I was especially impressed to see how well each strategy is discussed and adapted to the workplace. In a well-organized and highly visual manner, this book will assist everyone in increasing productivity, reducing barriers to effectiveness, and eliminating tired excuses we have all held onto for too long!"

WILMA FELLMAN, M.ED., LPC
Author of *Finding a Career That Works For You*
West Bloomfield, Michigan

"If you are like many people whose daily lives are surrounded by a multitude of distractions, you will simply love this book. Dr. Markel presents real-life examples of eight major types of distractions and how each can hinder a person from achieving life satisfaction and reducing stress. Each chapter is filled with proven strategies and techniques which are practical and simple to apply. I highly recommend this book for anyone who desires a lifetime of fulfillment with fewer distractions."

TERRY M. DICKSON, M.D.
The Behavioral Medicine Clinic of NW Michigan
Traverse City, Michigan

"Feeling distracted from your work? Procrastinating again? If so, read Dr. Geraldine Markel's newest book, *Defeating the 8 Demons of Distraction: Proven Strategies to Increase Productivity and Decrease Stress.* Distractibility plagues most of us; occasionally for some, constantly for others. Dr. Markel provides a thorough exploration of this common problem and addresses the different ways that people over-focus or under-focus. She provides universally helpful tools for focusing attention on essential tasks with ease and efficiency. Dr. Markel has written a great book with useful ideas and terrific solutions. Don't put it off any longer! Order this book immediately!!"

BRANDI ROTH, PH.D.
Psychologist, educator, and seminar presenter in Beverly Hills, California; author of *Choosing the Right School for Your Child, Secrets to School Success—Guiding Your Child Through a Joyous Learning Experience,* and *Role Play Handbook, Understanding and Teaching the New Reality Therapy, Counseling with Choice Theory*

"We live in a society where multitasking has become a respected social condition. A natural result from multitasking is stress and distractions. Stress and distraction can ruin your health. *Defeating the 8 Demons of Distraction* will help you understand how to get more peace and less stress into your life so you can live a happier, more productive life."

ED PRIMEAU
Primeau Productions
Troy, MI

"If you feel that you are not on top of things at work, home, or play then this book is for you. The author has focused in on areas that plague many of us in the form of demons that interfere with our ability to maximize our efforts. Here you will be able to identify these demons and more importantly, discover ways of getting rid of them on the way to a full, less distracted, and productive life. Read this book before you are distracted by anything else!"

PERCY BATES, PH.D.
Former Director, U.S. Office of Special Education Programs, Professor of Special Education and Director, Program for Educational Opportunity, University of Michigan

DEFEATING the 8 Demons of DISTRACTION

Also by the Author

BOOKS

Finding Your Focus: Practical Strategies for the Everyday Challenges Facing Adults with ADD (with Judith Greenbaum, Ph.D.)

Helping Adolescents with ADHD & Learning Disabilities: Ready-to-Use Tips, Techniques, and Checklists for School Success (with Judith Greenbaum, Ph.D.)

Performance Breakthroughs for Adolescents with Learning Disabilities or ADD: How to Help Students Succeed in the Regular Education Classroom (with Judith Greenbaum, Ph.D.)

Peterson's Parent's Guide to the SAT and ACT: Practical Advice to Help You and Your Teen (with Linda Bizer, Ed.D.)

Parents Are to Be Seen AND Heard: Assertiveness in Educational Planning for Handicapped Children (with Judith Greenbaum, Ph.D.)

PRODUCTS

Defeating the Demons of Distraction (Self-Coaching Card Deck)

Defeating the Demons of Distraction: 111 Ways to Improve Work/Life Performance and Decrease Stress (Booklet)

Parent's Guide to the SAT and ACT: Practical Advice to Help You and Your Teen (3 CD Package) (with Linda Bizer, Ed.D.)

Managing Your Memory (CD)

DEFEATING the 8 Demons of DISTRACTION

Proven Strategies to Increase Productivity and Decrease Stress

Geraldine Markel, Ph.D.

Ann Arbor, Michigan

Library of Congress Cataloging-in-Publication Data

Markel, Geraldine
    Defeating the 8 Demons of Distraction: Proven Strategies to Increase Productivity and Decrease Stress

ISBN 978-0-9791279-4-6
    1. Self-help for adults

Managing Your Mind® books and products are available at special quantity discounts to use as premiums and sales promotions, or for use in corporate training programs. For more information, please write to Geraldine Markel, Ph.D., 3975 Waldenwood Drive, Ann Arbor, MI 48105 or geri@managingyourmind.com or call 734 761 6498.

Demon art: Bidlack Creative Group, Ann Arbor, MI
Cover and interior design: Sans Serif, Inc., Saline, MI

Dedicated to my family,
the most desirable of all distractions

Contents

Acknowledgments

Medals of Honor to:

All those who were kind enough to share their *distraction goofs and glitches* for inclusion in this book.

Sheldon Markel, M.D., for his critical analysis, wit, love, and constant support.

Jane Heineken for her intelligence, eye for detail, humor, and fortitude.

Barbara McNichol for her masterful editing of the final draft.

Jeanne Ballew for her valuable and insightful editorial advice during the development of the first draft.

Friends, family, and colleagues, readers of earlier and later drafts, for their perceptiveness, laughter, and encouragement.

Carrie Wakulat, Lynn Nees, Carol Chan-Groening, Tiffany Dobson, Mary Morency, and Chris Bidlack of the Bidlack Creative Group for their out-of-the-box thinking coupled with competence.

Barbara Gunia and staff at Sans Serif, Inc. for their creativity and assistance.

Preface

Each of us can recall incidents when being distracted caused us negative consequences. In our roles as leaders, employees, family members, and of course, consumers, our lives are filled with distractions. Although this affects everyone today, some of us are by nature even more prone to be distractible. But even those with this tendency can learn better habits, use strategies to prevent succumbing to distractions, and prosper at work and home. My story is but one example.

Flaky but not stupid was the alias given to me by my friends. In fact, when they made "silly" mistakes and then found themselves in some humorous predicament, they would say they were "Pulling a Geri." That's the origin of the flaky part. However, when those same friends needed advice and observed my creative problem-solving skills, they realized that I was hardly stupid.

How does *flaky but not stupid* manifest itself? Here are some examples:

- As a new homemaker and wife, I made macaroni and cheese from scratch. In a rush, I missed the section that said the recipe was for six, so I doubled it for the two of us. I realized my error only after I used every new pot I owned. Faced with mounds of macaroni, my husband and I laughed, called all the neighbors, and had a party. That experience was funny.
- Later, as a new mother, I locked our baby in the car with the motor running. That experience was anything but funny. As my children got older, I was always rushing and late to pick them up from school or other activities.
- Rushing also caused travel problems. Once, leaving for a visit with family, I hastily stowed the luggage in the trunk of the car but then locked the keys in with it. Not

wanting to miss the plane, I asked a friend to drive us to the airport. I arrived in New York City with three kids, a box of crayons, two coloring books, and no clothes for any of us.

Moving from a carefree newlywed to mother, caregiver, and professional was arduous. As I matured, I began to understand the not-so-subtle and serious side of distractions and inattention to detail.

I also began to understand that some of my *habits* such as over scheduling and rushing were not only inconvenient but also inconsiderate. I came to realize that no amount of fun or apology makes up for a lack of consideration for a small child—or a busy spouse or a valued colleague. I didn't want the additional alias *absent-minded professor* applied to me after all I'd put into my career. I didn't have the luxury of distractibility and needed to stay on target whether at work or home. This was especially true after family tragedy struck and every ounce of our collective mental and emotional resources was needed to survive.

As an educational psychologist, I applied research regarding cognitive-behavioral strategies. It provided me with ways to help myself with family, career, and social life. In times of great trouble, these methods become a lifeline.

For the millions of people who are suffering the effects of everyday distractibility, this book provides a unique opportunity to enhance work/life satisfaction and decrease stress. I've learned to defeat my demons of distraction—and so can you.

Introduction

"Oh no! I put the $90,000 that was to cover the payroll checks in the money market account instead of the checking account. How could I have done that?"

Although Luda is a smart, determined, and competent woman, she gets distracted by her lighthearted conversation with the teller while doing her company's banking business. Even though her mistake is caught before any inconveniences (or costs!) occur, she suffers stress and embarrassment because of a silly error that was due to distraction.

For many of us, the boundaries between work and life have become blurred and evermore fast-paced technology interferes with our productivity and sense of well-being.

As we strive for peak performance, we are confronted by the threat of distraction in the form of short attention spans and poor concentration.

Are distractions causing you to make silly, costly, or even dangerous mistakes? As a result, do you feel stupid, embarrassed, or disappointed with yourself?

Does your crazy 24/7 life create conditions for the DEMONS OF DISTRACTION to march in and wreak havoc with your performance?

The word *demon* conjures up visions and feelings of danger, helplessness, and uncertainty. Is that how you feel when you make a mistake due to distraction or inattention? And, like Luda, do you ask, "How could I have done that?"

The 10 chapters that follow explore how to prevent, reduce, and avoid distraction. Each chapter offers sound, practical strategies—a plan of attack, if you will—for dealing with 8 common distractions and attention issues that are called the DEMONS OF DISTRACTION. Here's a brief description of the chapters.

Chapter 1: The 8 Demons of Distraction describes the demons that invade people's environments and interfere with their performance and productivity.

Chapter 2: Your Attention Reservoir and Arsenal helps you defend against distractions that deter you from living up to your potential. It also explains the importance of executive functions such as planning and organizing.

Chapter 3: Defeating the Technology Demon looks in-depth at the distractions triggered by cell phones and other electronic devices and shows you how to deal with the insidious effects of these so called time-savers.

Chapter 4: Defeating the *Others* Demon gives you techniques for getting others to respect your need for quiet time. It addresses how to deal with difficult people and turn negative interactions into positive ones.

Chapter 5: Defeating the Activities Demon provides you with scheduling techniques and helps you avoid procrastination and become more proficient at multitasking and making transitions.

Chapter 6: Defeating the Spaces Demon shows you how to create work/life environments that enhance your performance. This includes tips and techniques that will help you deal with the cubicle culture, home businesses, and working on the road.

Chapter 7: Defeating the Stress Demon describes common causes and symptoms of stress and provides you with everyday stress busters.

Chapter 8: Defeating the Fatigue Demon describes the prevalence and effects of fatigue and provides clinically tested methods to reduce fatigue and related distractions.

Chapter 9: Defeating the Illness and Medication Demon explains how illness and/or medication can interfere with attention and lead to distractibility. It includes guidelines to minimize the side effects of medication, steps for dealing with sudden illness, and ways to prevent paper pile-up during an illness.

Chapter 10: Defeating the Unruly Mind Demon reveals how daydreaming, hyper focus, and a racing mind can distract you from completing tasks and performing with speed and accuracy.

The final section—**Be Commander in Chief: Deploy These 10 Demon-Busting Strategies**—summarizes the 10 best strategies that you, as commander in chief of your life, can apply every day.

This book is intended for:

- high achievers who want to maintain their competitive edge as job challenges and work/life distractions increase
- people who want to upgrade their skills and attain new goals such as going back to school, seeking job promotions, or making career transitions
- people dealing with new technology, stress, illness, fatigue, rushing, and over-commitment
- people facing increasingly complex circumstances that feel overwhelmed and are worried about maintaining their performance, safety, and/or financial security

This book provides simple yet powerful strategies for people in every station in the workforce—CEOs to entry-level, independent professionals such as speakers, coaches, clinicians, and consultants, and homemakers; in short, people who pride themselves on their excellence and strive for continuous improvement.

Make use of the information in this book in any order that feels right for you. You may choose to start at the beginning and read straight through, or begin with the problem you're most interested in. Taking a simple, flexible approach to facing your particular demons fosters rapid improvement.

The chapters in this book feature real-life stories and step-by-step strategies that you can apply immediately.

Learn to defeat the 8 DEMONS OF DISTRACTION and you will:

✦ enhance your performance,

✦ reduce your stress,

✦ experience more peacefulness in your life, and

✦ likely boost your profits.

The 8 Demons of Distraction

Frank's story:

> "*I'm just not productive these days. I feel as if I'm under attack all day by people, calls, construction hassles, and added responsibilities. Even when I'm commuting, I can't relax. People are having fights on their cell phones or listening to their iPods at full volume.*
>
> *At home, I deal with a never-ending avalanche of interruptions and noise—kids, telephones, and televisions. It isn't until the 11 o'clock news comes on that I have some peace and quiet to concentrate on my personal correspondence. But, too frequently, I get distracted by surfing the Internet. By the time I finish doing that, it's well past a reasonable bedtime. Then I'm either keyed up or overwhelmed, and can't get to sleep. When the alarm rings early the next morning, I'm tired and discouraged about having to start the cycle all over again.*"

Do you see your performance deteriorating and realize that things are getting out of hand? Then you, like Frank, need a plan of attack to defend against distractions in your work/life.

This chapter introduces you to the problems posed by

distraction. You will probably recognize these 8 Demons of Distraction. If they're part of your work/life, you need to begin to address the problems they present.

Even the Best and the Brightest

Few people are immune to distractions. Even highly placed executives and professionals whose jobs require great amounts of attention and concentration are plagued by the Demons of Distraction.

In most cases, glitches happen when you are operating in overdrive and your mind is overloaded. When you're on the go all day and night dealing with people, problems, and responsibilities, your brain's circuits can't accommodate the overwhelming demand for attention energy—it's as if your mind is in one place and your body is in another.

Sometimes the distraction results in a harmless misadventure. Here's an example. One morning, a hurried physician looks for his favorite wristwatch. When he doesn't find it, he gives up and puts on a different one. Later that day, when he looks to see what time it is, he discovers that he's wearing two watches!

Many incidents are humorous and can be fluffed off. But unfortunately, distractibility during everyday activities begins to bleed into your professional life and has negative effects on your job performance or even your job security.

Carmen, a flextime MBA mom, puts her kindergartner on the school bus with her dress inside out. In her rush to get out the door to work, she grabs the hemorrhoid cream instead of her toothpaste tube and gets a nasty surprise. While sheepishly telling her co-workers about her hygiene error, she accidentally throws her cell phone on her desk and stuffs her stapler into her pocket as she leaves for an important conference. The distractions begin to have a more serious effect when she spouts the wrong figures in the meeting and forwards a confidential e-mail to the wrong parties.

It's easy to brush off such incidents as part of contemporary life, but to maintain your competitive edge, it's critical to take distractibility and inattention seriously. Do you believe that things are getting out of hand and feel that your performance is declining?

Have people made comments like this to you?

- "You need to pay better attention to where you put the receipts. How can we file the travel reports?"
- "You're moving from one thing to another but not finishing anything!"

Do you ask yourself questions like these?

- "How can I stick with a task and not get sidetracked?"
- "How can I better concentrate so I won't make so many foolish mistakes?"
- "How can I make sure that I don't make costly mistakes at work while I'm dealing with my illness?"

Why are distractions and attention-related problems epidemic, and what can we do about them?

What kinds of distractions are dragging you down? How can you defeat them so you can regain your cutting edge—and your confidence?

Your Foes: The 8 Demons of Distraction

Lurking around us is a squad of demons that distract us at work and at home. Any one of them can wield a powerful negative influence, but often they attack in combination, and that can exponentially increase their destructive abilities.

What can you do? First become aware of the roles they play in your life. Then deploy the strategies and tips in the chapters that follow. Have confidence that you *can* defeat this collection of demons!

1. The Technology Demon

The Technology Demon stays on duty all day and all night. It invites you to get lost in its mazes by working or playing long after it's appropriate or useful. In addition, when some device breaks down or needs maintenance, you might flounder and waste countless hours seeking help.

2. The Others Demon

As the name suggests, the *Others* Demon has many faces: co-workers, spouses, children, friends, and others who believe that you should be available 24/7—especially if you have a cell phone, e-mail, or an office at home.

When you're trying to complete a report, prepare for an important meeting, or just take a rest, others often think it is alright to ask questions such as, "May I ask you something?" or "May I have a minute of your time?" or "Do you mind if I come in?" Of course you mind, but you have a void in your working vocabulary: you can't say no.

3. The Activities Demon

This demon strikes when you inappropriately multitask, travel, rush, or work on tedious tasks. It's important to be aware of your vulnerability to distraction when you are doing too many things at once or beginning one activity before finishing another.

The Activities Demon strikes when you become heavily engaged in life's activities and events, both joyous and tragic. Life gets in the way of your already overcommitted schedule. Beware: you are especially vulnerable to distractions while preparing for special events such as holidays, births, graduations, weddings, or funerals.

4. The Spaces Demon

The Spaces Demon comes in many forms, distracting you with the sights and sounds where you work, live, or play. For example, cubicles at work aren't quiet; children at home rarely are quiet either. You feel as if you can't hear yourself think—and you are right. Consequently, you may feel confused and work at a slower pace because you're constantly retracing your steps. Failure to carefully plan the setting leads to errors and omissions.

5. The Stress Demon

The Stress Demon can be activated by internal or external triggers, robbing you of the psychic energy needed to pay attention. Being preoccupied by worries or stressed by events causes you to experience a kind of cognitive power outage.

When you're not mindful of the attention stealing effects of stress, you are set up to make mistakes. The greater the stress, the more vulnerable you are to mishaps or accidents.

6. The Fatigue Demon

The Fatigue Demon undermines the energy you need to focus and maintain concentration. You find that you don't even feel like starting tasks, especially if they're uninteresting or cumbersome. You may not be fully aware of fatigue's impact until mistakes are made, omissions are revealed, or accidents occur, making this demon extremely insidious.

7. The Illness and Medication Demon

This demon can rush into your life when you least expect it. Regardless of age or general physical health, illnesses and/or injuries sap your energy and increase your emotional vulnerability. For example, unless you've experienced it firsthand, you can't fully appreciate how tiring and anxiety-producing, mild but persistent pain can be. Additionally, you need to be aware of the possible effects of certain medications on your thinking, memory, or concentration.

8. The Unruly Mind Demon

The Unruly Mind Demon is a three-headed entity that manifests itself in several forms of excessive behavior: hyper focusing, racing mind, or daydreaming.

For some, the Unruly Mind Demon takes the form of hyper focusing, when you become so wrapped up in a task or activity that you ignore everything else. As a result you commit too much time and energy to what you are working on and neglect other things that need to be done and done well.

For others, this demon takes the form of a racing mind. You flit from one idea or activity to another, not taking the time to complete any one thing.

For still others, this demon takes the form of daydreaming. When daydreaming excessively, you're effectively *spaced out* and ignore the tasks at hand, and then abruptly you realize you've been in another world.

In summary, any demon of distraction can interfere with your attention and concentration; and more than one, in combination can severely debilitate your performance and sense of satisfaction.

Distraction Attacks: The Demons at Work

We easily accept "a slip of the tongue" but we're not so accepting of "a slip of the mind."

We may fail to pay attention to which medication to take or miss an important meeting on the calendar. When mishaps occur, we feel chagrined and worry that we're losing our minds. We have a choice: to react *productively* or *unproductively*.

The unproductive reaction to "slips of the mind" is both immediate and delayed. You can observe slippage in your performance and suffer the consequences of omissions or mistakes. Like Luda who made a $90,000 banking error, you can feel embarrassed but laugh it off.

Over time, if you have a number of similar experiences, you'd probably feel less productive than ever and begin to worry. Do you notice that worrying happens naturally if you usually take pride in your accomplishments but currently aren't performing up to your potential?

Over the long term, if you worry about your performance, that stress serves to undermine your confidence and inhibit your performance even more. You set in motion a downward spiral and increasingly feel helpless and hopeless.

But you can choose to have a productive response to your attention slippages.

First, when these incidents happen, take comfort in knowing you're not alone and that you're not lazy, crazy, or dumb. You've simply experienced a power outage—a temporary short circuit of the mind. In all likelihood, it resulted from one of these factors:

- a work/life imbalance,
- an absence of training to cope with today's uncertainties,
- poor attention habits, or
- simply too many distractions.

Second, decades of research have shown that poor attention habits can be broken and new, more productive habits can be learned. Yes, you *can* reduce distractions and make a better connection between positive attention and performance.
The good news is:

- You *can* reduce your vulnerability to distraction.
- You *can* tap into and bolster your attention reservoir.
- You *can* use an arsenal of research-based strategies to deal with distractions.
- You *can* realize greater competence, control, and confidence while confronting life's complexities.

When asked to reduce or better manage distractions, you might say, "Yes, but I've always been that way" or "What difference will it make?" or "I don't have time" or "I never had to pay attention to paying attention before—why should I now?"

Your response could be that today's world is more uncertain, complex, and changing than ever before. To be a high achiever, it's essential to employ all the skills you can master.

Continual learning and improvement is the name of the game for those who want to maintain their edge. That's why it's important to take an active role in defending against the 8 DEMONS OF DISTRACTION by using the strategies and tips presented in this book.

You might wonder, "What if none of these strategies work?" or "What's the difference between a person with bad attention habits and a person with Attention Deficit Disorder?" The symptoms of ADD or ADHD are *long-standing, pervasive,* and *chronic.* Some of the symptoms include short attention span, distractibility, disorganization, impulsivity, and time-management problems. Clusters of these symptoms interfere with realizing your potential at work, at home, and in social relationships. It is estimated that about 4% of the adult population, or 8 million people in the United States, have ADD (Greenbaum and Markel, 2006).

If you find that you have more than a few of these symptoms and they lead to serious consequences, such as poor performance evaluation, job loss, poor academic performance, or divorce, then you might consider contacting your physician or a psychologist for a screening or neuropsychological evaluation.

For more information, contact organizations such as ADDA (Attention Deficit Disorder Association, *www.add.org*) or CHADD (Children and Adults with Attention Deficit Disorder, *www.chadd.org*).

Review references such as Brown, 2005; Greenbaum and Markel, 2006; Hallowell and Ratey, 2005; Matlen, 2005; Rotz and Wright, 2005; and Solden, 2002 or other resources listed at the end of this book.

DEMON BUSTERS: Battle Plan

✦ Be more mindful of the part distraction plays in your life.

✦ Identify which of the 8 DEMONS OF DISTRACTION most commonly attack you.

✦ Adopt one or two strategies that help reduce distraction, enhance your performance, and reduce stress.

2

Your Attention Reservoir and Arsenal

Bill, a young man with a black leather attaché case by his side, is pacing with his cell phone in the vestibule of an upscale deli. He's wearing the garb of today's young professional: a blue, button-down shirt, a striped, red tie, and khaki twill pants. At first, he stands tall and straight, and says brashly, "Hi. It's Bill. Where are you? I thought our meeting time was 15 minutes ago." Then he wilts. Clutching the phone, he exclaims, "Yesterday? I don't understand. I wrote it in my planner for today!"

After the call has ended, he slinks to a nearby table to join his colleague and reviews his planner. With his head hanging low, he gasps and shields his brow with one hand. He moans, "I can't believe I did that. How stupid can I be? I wrote the appointment time for the wrong day. Now I'm nervous that I've messed up other appointments. I'll have to go over my calendar for the next two weeks to make sure it's right. You know, when I called the guy to ask where he was, he sounded annoyed. I'd better send him an e-mail to apologize."

How costly was Bill's error? Was this meeting to close a big deal? Was this a lost opportunity? Was this a first-time incident or does this missed appointment represent a negative pattern in his professional or personal life?

10

This chapter explores the costs of distractions and the need for greater mindfulness of the strengths that can help you access your attention reserves. You will discover a powerful arsenal of strategies and techniques to reduce distractions and improve your focus.

Costs of Distraction and Inattention

Whether occasional or common, incidents like this one cost time, money, and energy. They're not just inconveniences, they're certainly not humorous, and they could spell disaster for one's career. Given the complexity of his job and his goals, this young professional needs to tap into his natural reservoir of attention energy and employ a variety of strategies to defend himself against—and defeat—the DEMONS OF DISTRACTION.

If you don't pay careful attention to everyday happenings, you can endanger your safety or health. You know that. But do you realize the *degree* to which distractions and poor attention influence your effectiveness and satisfaction throughout the day?

Varied costs are attached to distractibility, inattention, and lack of concentration. Some are obvious, some more subtle.

Your Attention Reservoir

Have you ever found yourself making statements like these?

- *I felt as if I was running on empty—then I got my second wind.* Do you know that you have reserves of physical energy that you can always tap into?
- *I never thought I would learn how to use an Excel spreadsheet, but I did.* Do you know that with training you can ac-

cess greater thinking capacity? After all, it's said we use only about 10% of our total brain capacity.

- *I was drained. I couldn't come up with any new ideas for the project. The next morning I took a walk and thought of a whole new approach to the program.* Do you know that under the right conditions, you can harness your creativity?
- *I just couldn't think while trying to work in my cubicle.* Do you know that by using devices such as earphones, you can block out the chaos or find other ways to concentrate at work?

From these examples, do you see that when you reduce distractions and fatigue, you can better access your reserves of attention and use your mental energies?

Everyone has untapped attention potential. Imagine a large reservoir of attention energy that can be used to help you deal with the increasing demands of today's world. When you *pay attention to paying attention*, you quickly tap into your attention reserves to conserve, unleash, pace, and recoup your attention energy. And by doing so, you can optimize your performance.

You have reserves of mental energies that you can tap into to ward off the DEMONS OF DISTRACTION. When you have a greater awareness of this reservoir of attention, you can access it more systematically. You have the inner power to:

- Discover the specific eroding effects that distractions create within your work/life settings.
- Specify your natural vulnerabilities to certain distractions.
- Identify your natural learning and attention strengths.
- Exert greater control over the conditions that best reduce distractions.
- Schedule the times when you're most likely to have few distractions.

- Learn the conditions and consequences that allow for greater access and use of your attention resources.
- Apply techniques to conserve attention/energy such as taking breaks and dividing tasks into doable segments.
- Reach out and request help or support when your attention is at low ebb.

In addition, you can take comfort in the idea that you have untapped mental energy stored in your attention reservoir.

It's one thing to know you have such a resource. It is quite another thing to use it effectively.

Your Attention Arsenal of Strategies and Techniques

Self-awareness and self-regulation are the keys to winning the battle against the 8 DEMONS OF DISTRACTION. Like a military strategist, you first look at the overall problem, assess it, and then choose which strategies and techniques to deploy.

Your basic attention arsenal should contain these 8 strategies proven to be effective in regulating attention behavior:

1. Assessing Your Behavior

It's important to determine the *best* and *worst* times for you to pay attention. This way, you have a baseline from which you can analyze your behavior and develop a plan of action.

First, think of a situation in which you experience high focus, with few distractions.

Second, imagine a specific task you do when you best pay attention.

Third, imagine times during which you are less able or unable to pay attention.

Last, compare the positive and not-so-positive pictures. Then ask these questions:

- What is the ratio of my most-to-least productive situations?
- How frequently each day, week, or month am I distracted?
- Does this pattern contribute to feeling disappointed and frustrated with my performance?
- If I continue this pattern, what are the chances that I'll maintain my competitive edge, further develop my potential, expand my horizons, and enjoy peace of mind?

Clearly, if you're aware that distractions are interfering with your performance and potential, then make a plan to consciously tap into your attention reservoir and enhance your ability to pay attention.

You can arm yourself against distractions and enhance your performance.

2. Setting Goals

As the commander in chief of your mind, you can decrease distractions by (1) engaging in systematic planning and (2) monitoring and modulating your attention energy.

Research indicates that chances for success are enhanced when you follow these 6 goal-setting steps:

1. Identify a few relevant goals that are important to you.
2. Prioritize each goal according to its possible positive and negative consequences.
3. Make a plan to do the tasks associated with each of those goals.
4. Identify the most effective way to use or tap into your attention reservoir.

5. Monitor your progress. Are you accomplishing what you set out to do?

6. Change what you're doing if you are not realizing the rate or type of success you desired.

3. Monitoring Progress

Critical to success is collecting and using objective information about your progress. Why? It helps you decide if you should *maintain* or *modify* your behavior. This is called feedback.

The type of feedback you will use depends on your learning or attention style. For example, if reading and writing appeal to you, you might check off items you've written on a list. If you like visuals and numbers, you might track your progress on calendars or graphs. If you prefer more concrete indicators, you can give yourself a tangible reward.

> *Carl drops $5 into the "Attention Bank" every time he works on his tax return. He thinks of the time spent as "money in the bank." This reinforces his efforts and keeps him on track. He can even monitor his progress by actually counting his accumulated money.*

Gathering specific, timely, and relevant information about your progress will help you stay on track and make adjustments when needed.

4. Making Positive Statements to Yourself

Some people see an error and use it as an illustration of a character flaw or evidence of inadequacy. They engage in negative self-talk such as "I'm so dumb. I always do things like that. I knew I couldn't do it." This type of negativity shuts down all self-improvement efforts.

You've seen people view a mistake or lack of progress as a performance problem rather than a personality defect. They say things like "I missed the time I planned to write checks. What was it that caused this difficulty? How can I rearrange things to help me get done what I planned to do?"

Replace negative self-talk with productive self-talk. Why? Because positive self-talk shifts the behavior into a problem-solving arena. Once you define a problem out loud, you can devise a solution yourself or seek help.

Dealing with problems and solutions opens the doors to more optimistic and creative thinking.

5. Developing Automatic Behaviors

Habits and routines help develop automatic behaviors. You can repeat the same steps in the same sequence at the same time of day to reinforce a desirable routine. You can also structure your time, space, and rate of action.

Many people need to make a list of things they must *not* do when working. *Neil created the following "Don't" list to stop interrupting himself when working with power tools, especially when his young children were around.*

- *Don't answer the phone.*
- *Don't bring any food into the work area.*
- *Don't leave the work area without turning off power tools.*

Writing a list or plan brings any problem into better focus. If it's worth thinking about, it's worth writing about.

6. Making a Contract with Yourself

Developing contracts with yourself is an effective way to reduce distractions, gain better attention connections, and better employ your attention reservoirs. A contract is a formal agreement that includes a goal and expected outcome, a schedule, and a process or technique for achieving the goal. Your rewards will be realized when your goal is accomplished. The best contracts are specific and should involve small goals (or steps) relating to important issues. They should also have highly reinforcing consequences.

It's good to have social support even when you're self-contracting. Sharing your successes (as well as your difficulties) helps you to stay focused and find alternatives if things don't work out as planned.

7. Knowing How to Best Trigger Your Attention

In the military, the "Atten . . . *tion!*" command triggers an image of a soldier with erect posture, eyes looking straight ahead, arms at the sides, and heels together. To see someone at attention is to witness someone's mind and body at conscious alertness, totally ready for instruction and action.

In the animal world, a cat stalking its prey illustrates the attention connection posture. The cat employs a total focus of energy for action through its senses and bodily mechanisms.

Concentration means focusing mental powers on an object or task, being engaged in close or careful observation or listening. Once called to "Atten . . . *tion!*" you respond by saying something like "I'm all ears" or "I'll keep my eye on it" or "I'll be on the lookout."

Like the soldier or the cat, you can use your innate senses and preferred learning styles to create routines that help you become better aroused, alert, and focused. Tap into the attention triggers that fit with your learning style.

For example, if you learn best with visual aids, then write on Post-it notes of various sizes and colors. In addition, you can color code different files or highlight directions or use lighting devices such as automatic lamps or flashing lights.

If you learn best when you hear information, your attention may be best triggered by sound devices such as alarms, bells, and beepers.

If you're a hands-on or kinesthetic person, then your attention may be triggered by tactile devices such as vibrating watches or cell phones.

Your goal is to use your strengths to circumvent your vulnerabilities. If you have difficulty remembering numbers, for example, admit it. To compensate, carry paper and pencil with you to jot down information like telephone numbers and directions.

Certain learning strengths involve specific triggers that activate your attention and learning. Use these triggers to help manage yourself and the environment around you.

8. Using the Stop, Look, and Listen Technique

Use this handy technique whenever a slipup occurs. Also use it when you feel tired, ill, stressed, or preoccupied with a particular life circumstance such as a trip or wedding. Make this technique part of your everyday routine and you will ensure that you're effective when completing tasks of personal or financial importance (e.g., legal, tax, health) or dangerous activities (e.g., using power tools, driving heavy equipment).

Stop: Take a time-out for half a minute or even a few full minutes. Allow your mind and body to relax and refocus on the task at hand.

Look: Be vigilant about the conditions under which you are to perform or complete a task. What materials are needed? What are possible dangers or pitfalls?

Listen: Give yourself instructions about what to do and what not to do. When you talk to yourself, you will focus better and listen more carefully. You will become less distracted by outside noises or intrusive thoughts.

It's like a mini-refresher course you tap into any time of the day! Stop, look, and listen to what's going on around you.

Use your arsenal of strategies to become more mindful of the conditions, consequences, and costs of work/life distraction and begin to address them.

DEMON BUSTERS:
Reserves and Ammunition

✦ You have a deep reservoir of attention energy available—tap into it!

✦ Experiment with various ways to better trigger and access your attention.

✦ Employ an arsenal of tools and strategies to help in your struggle to reduce distraction.

The **TECHNOLOGY DEMON** is on the prowl day and night. It invites us to get lost in a maze of texting, chatting, surfing, and gaming long after it's appropriate or useful.

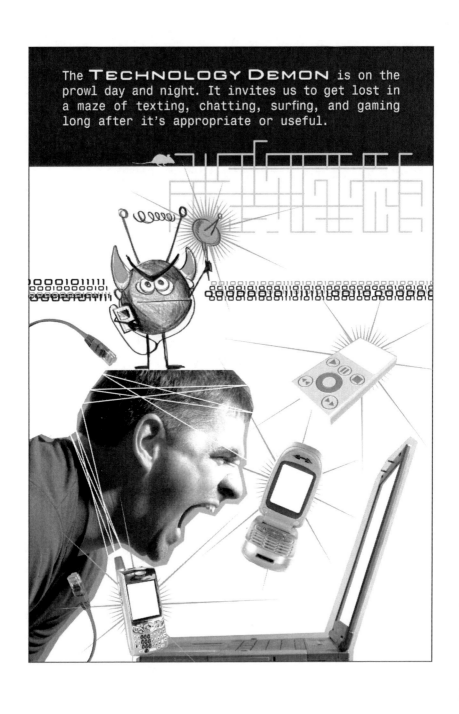

3

Defeating the Technology Demon

1944: *A reporter is covering a war in France. He carries a pen and pad.*

2004: *A reporter trudges along a dirt road in a third world country. Among other supplies and accessories, she carries:*

> *Laptop*
>
> *Blackberry (Personal Digital Assistant or PDA)*
>
> *PDA charger*
>
> *Cell phone*
>
> *Cell phone charger*
>
> *Digital camera*
>
> *Digital camera charger*
>
> *Digital video camera*
>
> *Digital video charger*
>
> *Assorted cords, cables, adapters, batteries, and cases*

The headline describing this reporter's experience is "Be Prepared; One Possible Cost of Mobile Technology: A Tired, Aching Back." (Seelye, *New York Times*, January 29, 2004). Although she gathers and sends information and visuals more quickly than the reporter of yesteryear, the heavy, awkward equipment slows her down. It frequently breaks down and, if lost, can't be easily replaced. Plus, don't you think dealing with the various devices can easily distract a reporter from her primary reporting tasks?

It's not only reporters who are feeling the psychological and physical impact of today's technology mixed with a fast-paced life. Many of us load ourselves down with devices that bombard our ears and eyes with rings, alarms, voices, music, and visual stimulation.

Consider these facts:

- An estimated 229 million Americans subscribe to cell phone service, bringing conversations into the public domain at an ever increasing rate (CTIA-The Wireless Association, 2006).
- Many Americans have more than one telephone line. Considering there may be several phones in the home, two or three lines can be ringing at once.
- Loud, disruptive music, movies, or talk show chatter can be blaring from several sources in public places.

Many of us have slowly but consistently incorporated a variety of these technical wonders into the fabric of our lives. But each time-saving device requires technical skills to run and maintain. Few of us, however, have adjusted our attention skills so we can effectively manage these innovations and avoid their distracting effects.

What's the danger in getting distracted? It can result in a variety of consequences, some severe. For example, if we lose our focus while driving or using power tools, we might cause an accident.

This chapter reveals how the Technology Demon can impact the quality of your life and shows how to defend against its perils.

Plugged-In, Tuned Out while Driving

Steering the car with one hand, Nick jots down a phone number while on his hands-free cell phone. His iPod is connected to his audio system and he's whizzing down the expressway at seventy-five miles per hour somewhat oblivious to his surroundings.

Then he hears a siren wailing behind him. For a second, he's confused. This doesn't make sense . . . he rarely speeds on this road. But one glance at his speedometer reveals the truth, and he realizes too late that his distraction with the cell phone is going to cost him big-time.

As he watches the officer approach his car, he notices for the first time that he sped right through the middle of a construction zone. He's busted.

Nick thinks he's safer on the road because he uses a hands-free cell phone. In fact, he's less safe because rather than using two hands on the wheel he tries to write notes while driving. The distractions caused by technology, in this case a cell phone and iPod, cost him.

"Inattention blindness" is a term used by University of Utah researchers Strayer, Drews, and Johnston (2003) to describe what happens when you are talking on a phone while driving: although your gaze is directed at objects in the driving environment, you may fail to see them because your attention is taken up by your conversation. Motorists are slower to react to driving situations while engaged in cell phone conversations; therefore they are more likely to have accidents. Unfortunately, this holds true even when the driver is using a hands-free headset.

Yes, you increase your risk of causing an accident when you use a cell phone while driving, especially in heavy traffic, construction zones, rough weather, or poor surface conditions. Because of this, cell phone use while driving has become a legislative matter: many

officials think it should be banned altogether. Do you ever jeopard-
ize the lives of children you drive in your car because you're distracted as you use a cell phone?

Do you need a law to help you deal with the distractions
posed by cell phones? Or can you begin to manage this problem
yourself?

Here are 6 ways to reduce distractions while driving:

1. Check that you've fastened your safety belt before starting
   your car—always.

2. Create guidelines for your cell phone use. For example, limit
   using your phone to incoming calls only. For outgoing calls,
   limit them to numbers on automatic dial, wear a headset,
   only discuss logistics, and avoid emotional or important
   conversations. Be ready to hang up or pull off to the side of
   the road if the conversation takes a serious turn. Even when
   using automatic dialing, it's easy to miss a road sign or drift
   into a neighboring lane. The inner speech and vision used
   to monitor or anticipate drivers' actions (including your
   own) are simply not present.

3. Keep your cell phone in a visible and accessible place
   while driving. Your attention is quickly affected when you
   hear the ringing of your cell phone and must search for it
   in a purse, briefcase, backpack, or diaper bag.

4. Organize and make accessible your supplies such as tis-
   sues, maps, pencils, paper, CDs, and garbage container.

5. Park your car if you need to eat something or groom
   yourself. You'll avoid the dangerous consequences of burns
   from hot coffee or a poke in the eye from a mascara wand,
   not to mention getting stains from ketchup, mustard, or ice
   cream.

6. Set rules for appropriate car behavior so you don't have demands for your attention from noisy or fighting children (or adults). If you must tend to children in the car, pull off the road. Keep a tote bag of activities, books, snacks, and games for traffic tie-ups or other delays.

Plugged-In, Tuned Out while Walking

Tanya is trying to make her way down crowded Fifth Avenue in New York City. Among the pedestrians who bump and jostle her, many are plugged into not one but multiple devices used in ways that could overstimulate their senses and distract them.

- *An older gentleman wearing a white lab coat has three beepers and a cell phone. He is also punching information into his PDA as he walks. He stumbles and almost falls.*
- *A woman in a suit is wearing ear pieces attached to different cell phones and is arguing with someone through one of them.*
- *A messenger wearing Rollerblades is creating a bottleneck as he leans against the wall, listening to his MP3 player and typing on a laptop computer.*

Do you feel lost without your iPod or cell phone? If so, have you adjusted your attention so you can effectively manage these innovations and avoid getting distracted?

It's easy to be distracted when plugged into audio devices. You can miss cues and signals, misinterpret directions, and lose focus. If you set the volume too high on an audio player, you can damage your hearing.

In addition, today's current lifestyle allows technology to contribute to the attention drain in this culture.

There is no downtime.

In fact, the majority of adults and children seem to be scheduled and busy every hour of the day with no respite. On a long-term basis, receiving stimuli all the time and feeling overscheduled or overwhelmed are major barriers to high levels of focus and performance.

Go for an Electronic Lockdown

Suppose you need to write a report but you keep getting distracted by calls and e-mails you receive. *Stop the interruptions!* You can disarm the Technology Demon with an electronic lockdown. Here are some tips:

- Estimate the amount of time you need and then shut off all equipment except the one device that you need to use.
- Turn on the telephone answering machine and turn off the ringer.
- Place the cell phone where you won't see any lights or text messaging.
- Turn off the music and post a sign on your computer that says "NO INTERNET NOW!"

This electronic lockdown is guaranteed to reduce distractions and increase your ability to focus on the task at hand.

When Your Strength Becomes Your Weakness

Steve is exceedingly bright and creative. He enjoys surfing the Internet and discovering new ideas. As a word or concept pops into his mind, his fingers tap him into uncharted territory. Four or more hours can fly by.

Unfortunately, these Internet explorations distract him from completing his projects. On the one hand, Steve is an "idea generator" at a public relations firm, so he needs to keep abreast of new developments. On the other hand, he still has to complete his projects.

When not carefully controlled, Steve's curiosity, usually his strength, becomes a weakness. The Technology Demon erodes his performance and potential. If you're like Steve, you can follow these suggestions to avoid letting the Internet distract you from your performance goals.

- Use the "First You Work and Then You Play" rule. Do your work first. If you need information from the Internet or another resource, leave blank spaces until you complete a portion of your work. After you complete a certain number of tasks or work for a prescheduled amount of time, then use the Internet (or games or other entertaining computer features).
- Allot special times for exploration and discovery outside of your work environment. Keep a list of ideas or words. Schedule a time each day or week for *free play*. You can prioritize and schedule time for each topic.
- Set a time limit for Internet use. Use a time device such as a kitchen timer, wristwatch alarm, or handheld device to help you enforce the limit.
- Create a file system for hard-copy reprints or create folders for information you collect from the Internet.
- Be honest. In regard to the Internet, are you using your time wisely or are you experiencing diminishing returns? If you are allowing technology to distract you from your goals, you have the power to change.

Schedule Technology Time

Hal can easily lose time when he answers his e-mail. As a manager, he may receive 60, 90, or more messages a day. He's tried answering them before work, after work, and during lunch, but he's always behind.

Given the crisis nature of his job, his boss and staff believe he should always be available. But although part of his job is "putting out fires," he also needs to write reports, review data, and develop programs. He feels exasperated and inadequate.

Finally, Hal devises a plan to schedule e-mail responses throughout the day. He allots 20 minutes of alternating hours beginning at 8:00 AM. Then he tells his staff he'll be testing this schedule for the next few weeks. He's not sure how well the plan will actually work but at least having a plan helps him to feel more in control and less frazzled.

You, too, can set up a plan. When you stick to it, you'll feel more in control of your time and activities.

Organization as a Defense against the Technology Demon

In his home office, Eduardo is deep into an Excel spreadsheet as he puts on the finishing touches for a financial report. He has completely forgotten that a new desk is scheduled to arrive in 10 minutes.

He hurriedly pulls out the plugs and cords of the computer, scanner, fax, printer, phone, answering machine, router, and various connections for the camera and audio. After his desk gets situated, he stares with horror at the mound of unlabeled paraphernalia. It takes Eduardo and his wife Marilyn a full day to reassemble their equip-

ment. Of course, they argue, with Marilyn saying, "Why weren't the cords labeled? Where are the manuals? Why is this taking so long?" By the end of the day, there is no communication occurring in this office, either between devices or spouses.

The Technology Demon is at Work

Eduardo and his wife Marilyn are distracted from their work. They need better organization to prevent losing time and energy looking for manuals and related matter. Eduardo's lack of planning and organization wastes time and energy and triggers stress.

Try these 8 tips for organizing your technology toys and preventing technology-related disasters and distractions:

- Use an accordion-pleated file or file drawer to store all manuals and warranties.
- Use a plastic box or drawer to store software related to your equipment or accessories such as camera, video, scanner, router, antivirus program.
- Keep a notebook with plastic sleeves to store instructions about dealing with special problems or accessing technical support.
- Label each cord as soon as it's purchased and installed.
- Keep all computer-related resource books on the same shelf for quick reference.
- Allot space or drawers in which to keep supplies such as toner, paper, and computer cleaning supplies.
- Allot storage space for materials and supplies required for small equipment such as microcassette recorder tape, MPG minidisks, microphones, chargers, cords, batteries.
- Label all small equipment such as your camera, laptop, and iPod with your name, phone, and/or e-mail address.

Conquer Computer Clutter

Although technology allows for easy access and collection of information, you can suffer from too much of a good thing.

Do you find yourself searching through your documents for files or distracted by outdated reports, misplaced files, or inaccurately labeled files? You can become frustrated and overwhelmed because you can't find what you need. Or you can reduce distractions by clearing the computer clutter weekly or monthly.

Make an appointment with yourself so you can accomplish these tasks:

- Weed out outdated material saved from the Internet.
- Organize files into folders in the "My Documents" section of your hard drive.
- Back up work on flash memory or a disk.
- Throw out diskettes, CDs, or DVDs that you no longer need.
- Keep children's software in a separate section and give away items you no longer use.
- Create a hard copy of critical e-mail addresses. Maintain a hard-copy list of log-in, membership, password, and phone number for stores, organizations, or networking groups.
- Keep an extra supply of labels to affix on discs or CDs.

Avoid the Dollar Drain

Technology brings into your home a steady, readily accessible stream of activities that can drain your dollars and can sometimes lead to disastrous results. Recent reports indicate a sharp rise in gambling, gaming, and shopping via computers, television, and handheld devices. Because participating from home is so easy, many Internet users are experiencing even more serious gambling/spending addictions than people who frequent casinos or shopping malls. Particularly frightening is the fact that virtual gambling and gaming sites offer easier credit than regular venues. Among the most vulnerable to these addictions are teens and young adults, who often have the tech savvy to load thousands of dollars onto their parent's credit card accounts before they're caught. Even the more mature person can be sucked into the Home Shopping Network frenzy or the eBay abyss. Since there is no physical exchange of cash for merchandise, virtual purchasers are distracted by the excitement of the process and lose focus on the actual time or money being spent.

Here are some tips to avoid being seduced by the Technology Demon into wasting time and accumulating debt due to excessive electronic spending:

- Keep track of the actual time and dollar amounts you spend each day or week on such activities.
- Set time and spending limits and do not use credit to finance such activities.
- Watch for warning signs such as lying to others about the time or money you spend on computer gambling, gaming, or shopping.
- Reach out for expert help. If you think you have a problem, you probably do. Contact a therapist or agency online such as *www.GamblersAnonymous.org, www.shopaholics anonymous.org,* or *www.olganonboard.org.* For example, the latter describe themselves as a 12-step, self-help organization and Web site dedicated to helping those addicted to computer/video/console/on line games.
- Safeguard your computer passwords and credit card

accounts so that teens or other family members can't develop or feed their own excessive behavior.

Manage the Technology, Manage the Distractions

Like every expensive or important aspect of life, technology must be managed—and you're the manager in charge.

Follow these 5 steps for managing technology and reducing distractions:

1. Take responsibility to learn how to care for equipment and make minor repairs (e.g., getting back online after a power outage), have on-call technical support numbers posted for software difficulties, and find a reliable technical support person or service that comes on-site. Allot time each week or month to update software programs.

2. Learn a little every week. Most of the problems users have with e-mail or software programs stem from misuse and misunderstanding. Trial and error is often the least effective and most time-consuming way to fix problems. Instead of spinning your wheels, take a course, get an easy-to-read manual, call a friend, or use technical support services to continually upgrade your skills.

3. Set up a schedule to accommodate different users if computers are shared.

4. Keep a log of common problems and solutions.

5. Assess your skills and bad habits, and make a commitment to improve.

Technology should help rather than hinder you. When you do not adequately manage your equipment, software, or gadgets, you create unnecessary and unnerving distractions and lose time and energy.

DEMON BUSTERS:
On the Offensive against the
Technology Demon

Enhance your experience with technology by:

✦ Increasing your awareness

✦ Improving your skills through education

✦ Developing specific strategies to reduce distractions

✦ Improving the organization of how you store your technology toys and accessories

The **OTHERS DEMON** has many faces: co-workers, bosses, significant others and/or children who feel we should be available 24/7. When we can't stop interruptions, set boundaries, or say no, opportunities for creativity are lost.

4

Defeating the "Others" Demon

Many people know what they need to do to decrease distractions, increase attention, and improve performance at work, home, or school. Almost in the same breath, however, they give you a laundry list of excuses regarding *why* they can't change.

The first line-up of excuses includes these:

- *"My staff is always asking questions."*
- *"There are too many interruptions when I'm working."*
- *"Someone is always distracting the group during meetings."*
- *"The kids are calling me all day long."*
- *"I'm taking a course online but those text messages and e-mail pop-ups are driving me crazy."*

Obviously, in certain situations, you have little or no control. But you do have much more influence than you think. You have rights as well as responsibilities that influence the what, when, where, how, and with whom you work.

This chapter identifies major interruptions posed by others and provides you with tips and suggestions to defend against these distractions at work and at home.

Monitor Distractions from Others

Information about the kind and number of distractions from others that occur in a day or week can pinpoint where you need to take action.

Create a list by identifying *who* to deal with first and when and where to deal with them. Select the easiest person to deal with first to practice your skills. If you already know *who* presents the most distractions, then monitor *when* and *how frequently* they occur.

Use Assertive Actions to Reduce Distractions

Assertiveness is the skill of standing up for your rights and expressing what you need honestly and politely. It conveys the idea that your needs and feelings are as important as others' (Alberti and Emmons, 2001).

If you are aggressive, then you tend to act on the principle that *your* needs or wants come before those of others. If you are passive, you're likely to act on the principle that *everyone else's* needs come before yours.

Defending against the distractions caused by others requires neither aggressive nor passive behavior; it calls for assertive behavior. If you know what conditions best contribute to positive attention and peak performance, you have a right to ask for or arrange those conditions.

Whether you're a manager or a staff member, a homemaker or a home worker, you also have a right and responsibility to say "no" to unnecessary interruptions.

Are you, like most people, more assertive in your thoughts

than in your actions? Assertiveness means you're active in your attempts to defend against distractions from others.

Assertiveness also means that you:

- Say what you want or need and state why.
- Look directly at the person who is distracting you.
- Assume a positive body position including a straight body trunk with open arms and hands.
- Have an "I mean business" facial expression.
- Be polite but firm. Ask people to stop the behaviors that interrupt or distract you.
- Thank them if they comply and remind them if they don't.

Deal with Distractions from Those Nearest and Dearest

It's difficult to know what to do when co-workers, friends, or family members constantly interrupt you. They make comments such as:

- *"May I ask you a question? It will only take a minute."*
- *"Can you help me with this?"*
- *"Wait 'til you hear this story."*
- *"Are you working?"*

They may not understand the *degree* to which their interruptions have a negative effect on your performance.

Often, others hold a mistaken assumption that they should have access to you all the time—in person or via the phone. Unintentionally, the people in your life break your train of thought and make it difficult to get back on task.

However, you *can* actively and consciously influence their behavior so you can be more productive. Small changes can result in large improvements.

Experiment with the following 10 guidelines:

1. Politely deny others' requests to interrupt you when you're working. (Say: "I'm really sorry but I can't talk now. I wish I could.")

2. Work with them to set a time to deal with their questions or concerns. (Say: "Can you e-mail or call me in an hour?")

3. List times and conditions in which it's okay to disturb you (Say: "Call only if it is serious or an emergency.")

4. Rearrange the setting in which you work to reduce easy access to you. If they invade your space, get up and gently walk them out of the room, then suggest an alternate time to talk.

5. Create a routine; set a particular time to work on tasks requiring full attention.

6. Express your gratitude to others for not interrupting you.

7. Use your answering machine or voice mail to do what it's made to do—record incoming calls. Turn off the ringer and forget about the phone until you complete your work.

8. Temporarily switch off the function that signals the arrival of new e-mail.

9. Use a sign or symbol of some kind to indicate that you're unavailable. For example, hang a picture of a clock on your door, on the back of your chair, or on the side of the computer that indicates that you are "on the clock" or under a deadline. Be sure to convey to others what your selected symbol means.

10. Ask for time to think things over if someone interrupts you with a request.

Deal with the Distraction of Inconsiderate Callers

Sitting in a quiet, intimate restaurant, a couple is discussing their upcoming wedding. The romantic atmosphere is broken when the cell phone at the next table loudly plays the introductory notes of Beethoven's Fifth Symphony. The person who answers the phone is oblivious to those around him as he relates portions of his raucous conversation and off-color jokes to the rest of the table at full volume.

Have you ever heard more than you want to know about the personal life of a stranger via his or her end of an inappropriate cell phone conversation? According to one survey, cell phone chatter annoys almost two-thirds of Americans (Whitmore, 2005) and poses problems in offices as well as homes.

Be it strangers, co-workers, friends, or family, to lessen the problem of inconsiderate callers, you can:

- Ask people to call during your regular waking hours, for example from 8:00 AM to 10:00 PM.
- Announce times when you don't wish to receive calls.
- Post a reminder for people to silence the ringer and set it to vibrate before attending meetings.
- Put up posters and send reminders to tell people not to shout when they're on their phones.
- Use features like caller ID, call waiting, call forwarding, and voice mail to reduce interruptions.
- Remind others not to discuss confidential or personal business in public places.

Sometimes, your nearest and dearest are those doing the most distracting things, as these examples show:

- *Connie's husband is newly retired. On average, he calls her 14 times a day—on her way to work, during meetings, lunch, and so forth.*

- *Roger's girlfriend sends him text messages all day long. She's irritated when he doesn't respond, but he's a salesman and can't reply during meetings and while traveling.*

- *Josh, a single parent of two teenagers, receives calls from them all day long. When he tries to impose limits on their calls, they say he doesn't care about them.*

- *Sally's kids and husband seem to want to talk to her only when she's on the telephone. They interrupt her when she is getting directions, asking for financial information, or contacting repair services.*

Connie, Roger, Josh, and Sally need to be assertive and extremely diplomatic. Frequently, love and logic don't mix.

If you deal with similar situations, use this step-by-step strategy:

1. Choose an appropriate time and place to discuss the situation the caller is phoning about.

2. Restate your love and loyalty. For example, you can say something to the effect of: "I love you and want to be in contact. I enjoy and look forward to the time we have together when I'm not working or doing business."

3. Talk about the difficulty of "too much of a good thing" given your job responsibilities.

4. Distinguish between *needing* versus *wanting* to talk.

5. Provide options and ask for suggestions to communicate at more appropriate times.

6. Impose a limit—at least for a trial run. If dealing with small children, have a practice run. Show them how you

will signal them, what they should do, and how you will reinforce their considerate, nondistracting behavior.

Take Charge of Distractions When Working at Home

If your business is home-based, you're not alone. A recent report indicates that the home *is* the office for half of all U.S. companies (Wyss, 2006).

Business people who have home offices often have difficulty concentrating and staying on task because others interrupt them. If you work at home, you see that some believe you're not really working, especially if you're wearing sweat pants. Family, friends, delivery personnel, telemarketers, and pets think they can interrupt you without even hesitating. Watch out! Having unstructured time and inconsistently imposed rules contribute to your vulnerability to others' distractions when working at home.

Experiment with these ways to better manage your work environment at home:

- Separate your work space from your living space. Even a screen or curtain will do.
- Set up a business-like atmosphere. Post a sign "This is the office of (name of firm)." Make it clear that work is work whether you're in an office or in a home.
- Post business hours. "This office is open from __ to __ and closed for lunch."
- Post rules or limits for interruptions. Identify times when you will take breaks and be available.
- Have a family meeting to discuss the importance of having a distraction-free work setting. Some guidelines include: moderate volume for music, no yelling to get

someone's attention, the dog is not allowed in the office.

- Identify two to four significant distractions presented by others and discuss ways to avoid them.
- Alert friends that you don't want them to "touch base" during business hours. Give them times you're available. Record this message on your home and/or cell voice mail.
- Post signs for delivery people. For example you can write: "Please do not ring door bell; leave all deliveries."
- Hold regular family meetings to share the successes realized due to reducing distractions. Deal with thorny issues that have arisen at the meeting.
- Provide compliments, privileges, or small gifts to those who respect the limits you set.

Defend against Distractions Triggered by Conflict

Conflicts and the emotions that go with them can be distracting when you want to work. Even in the case of minor disagreements, dealing with the conflict quickly, honestly, and firmly reduces stress. However, that's easier said than done. Although you may want to act assertively, you may feel unsure of what to say or how to say it. If you don't say anything, the danger is becoming preoccupied with what you could or should have said. The problem doesn't go away and you explode.

What can you do instead?

First, take an emotional time-out and then make a plan. (Better yet, preplan how to react to conflicts if you can. It will help you act more assertively and avoid unnecessary outbursts.)

Second, prepare for a difficult interaction by visualizing it. Write out what you want to say and then ask a friend, counselor, or human resource advisor to help you refine the wording.

Jeff wants to be "nice" but he is furious with a co-worker who constantly interrupts him when he's writing reports. Instead of "telling him off," he writes a script for himself. He practices each part of the script and then selects a quiet, non distracting location to meet.

When Jeff wasn't sure what his script should contain, he went to the library and found a book to guide him, *Asserting Yourself: A Practical Guide for Positive Change* (Bower & Bower, 2004). In this book, four steps are described for dealing with these kinds of situations:

1. Describe the situation: *"I need to have some uninterrupted time to finish this report. You've been popping in and out to ask questions even though I gave you the manual."*

2. Express your feelings: *"I'm frustrated and worried that the report won't be finished on time and that I'll make mistakes."*

3. Specify what you want: *"I want 30 minutes of 'think time' so I can finish this task with the accuracy that's required."*

4. Talk about positive and/or negative consequences: *"This report is to be presented at the staff meeting. An accurate report reflects well on all of us in this department. If you have questions, I'll be available to discuss them after the meeting."*

Because it is so difficult to confront conflict, it is important to visualize the situation and rehearse prior to dealing with the actual situation.

Ensure Uninterrupted Break Time

Brenda is the VP of a major health care provider during the most hectic of times—the company's annual audit. Taking breaks is important so she can stay alert, but she practically has to close herself in a closet to take a breather.

During one of her breaks, a co-worker follows her into the bathroom and knocks on her stall wanting to ask a question! Brenda thinks, "This is the last straw!"

Breaks are necessary for achieving positive work flow. In fact, U.S. law requires that workers take two 15-minute breaks during an eight-hour shift. Research studies indicate that taking breaks is critical for preventing computer-related injuries and to facilitate learning, retention, motivation, and focus (McLean et al., 2001).

The ideal "real" break is scheduled and refreshing. It allows for renewed energy and time to access your attention reservoir. Then you can return to your task with better focus and the fortitude to deal with frustrations that may arise.

Interrupted breaks, like interrupted sleep, can do more harm than good. Rather than lowering your stress, an interruption can raise it! Your right and responsibility is to plan your breaks (e.g., at least 5 minutes every 30 to 60 minutes), using them to rest, reduce stress, and disallow others from interrupting you.

Use these assertiveness skills to ensure uninterrupted breaks:

- Insist on taking your breaks; don't skip them!
- Set the stage: post a humorous reminder about the necessity of breaks.
- Discuss how to enforce uninterrupted break time at staff or family meetings.
- Post times when you plan to take breaks.

Manage Distractions Triggered by "Difficult" People

Unfortunately, interactions with a handful of people can frequently be disturbing and distracting. If you need to reduce such distractions, an active and assertive plan can help. Try these actions to reduce distractions from "difficult" people:

- Identify specifically how and why these "difficult" people irritate and distract you.
- Reach out to trusted colleagues or experts to help you analyze the situation and make a plan of action.
- Deal with specific situations or behaviors, especially if their distractions impose a significant barrier to your work/life performance.

It isn't easy to embark on a plan of action. You may feel more comfortable if you have guidelines. To create a new beginning with a "difficult person" follow these 8 steps:

1. Identify positive aspects of the "difficult" person.

2. Consider the personality style of the person. For example, compared to you, are they more of a numbers person, a talker, or a doer? Ask yourself, "Are my expectations realistic?"

3. Ask about this person's goals and priorities—and listen carefully to the answers.

4. Pinpoint your mutual interests, goals, and priorities. Ask yourself, "How can this person's style or strength help me or my situation?"

5. Determine and explain the ways you can best work or interact together.

6. Identify positive consequences for making this effort.

7. Make an extra effort to be friendly, kind, and/or empathetic—even when you'd rather not.

Try this approach several times. If you still can't find a point of connection, then avoid this person.

Cope with Distractions Triggered by Caretaking

Roger, a widower, runs a busy chiropractic clinic. Every morning he stops at his mother's home to check on her and her aides. As he walks into his office, he's thinking about which therapist is scheduled to go to her home next.

Since his mother's stroke, Roger's days are filled with making arrangements for her care, talking to physicians and getting calls from other family members who have opinions but not much else. Even when others help, (for example when his kids do the grocery shopping), he never feels like enough is being done.

Soon scheduled to go on vacation, Roger is thinking of canceling it. But his children are furious with him for even considering that option. They say he needs and deserves a rest.

Roger, like countless others in today's society, is continually distracted by caretaking responsibilities and interactions with caretakers and family members.

Many people in their 30s and 40s are raising their children while helping their parents or grandparents in their later years. It doesn't get less complicated over time. Many people in their 50s and 60s are responsible for caring for ill parents while being concerned with their adult children's situations, including childrearing and divorce. People like Roger get caught in the middle, meeting the needs (and wants) of themselves, their children, and their aging parents.

When it comes to the distractions related to caretaking, assertiveness means defining how you will fulfill your primary roles and setting your limits. What is reasonable? Unfortunately, that's not always easy to define. If you face this dilemma, consider meeting with a geriatric social worker, family therapist, and/or family physician to help define "reasonableness" in your situation.

Once you've determined your boundaries, stick with them!

DEMON BUSTERS: Marshaling Your Forces against the *Others* Demon

To defend against the distractions and interruptions of others at work or home and to avoid being vulnerable to poor performance, you can:

* Assertively stand up for your right to privacy, focus, and uninterrupted time.

* Impose limits on those near and dear to you.

* Identify your times of availability with co-workers or others at work.

* Deal with "difficult" people in respectful but assertive ways.

* Specify ways that others can *help* rather than *hinder* your efforts.

The **ACTIVITIES DEMON** attacks us when we inappropriately multitask, travel, rush, or face tedious, difficult tasks. The emotionality of events like holidays makes us easy prey for distractions.

5

Defeating the Activities Demon

Rick is an automotive engineer, newly promoted, and transferred to a different office. He should be enjoying his new status but he can't seem to get on track. He describes his problems: "Multitasking is making me crazy. There are constant changes in the product line and software programs. It's difficult to concentrate on exactly what I have to do and how to do it. And they're always adding rush jobs. In meetings, we keep going in circles without resolving anything. I feel as if there's no light at the end of the tunnel."

Do any of these statements sound familiar? If you're like Rick, you're experiencing increasing pressures to do more types of tasks and activities and confronting continuous demands to do more than one task at a time.

This chapter provides strategies to help you examine when and when not to multitask, investigate ways to minimize distractions, and rearrange schedules to improve performance. In addition, this chapter discusses activities such as rushing or special life events that make us especially vulnerable to distractions. With increased awareness and strategy, it is easier to complete tasks on time with accuracy and completeness.

Assertiveness: Dealing with Task-Related Demons

Assertiveness skills can help you deal with the demons that plague you when you try to complete tasks. To be assertive means that you ask for:

- Clear directions
- Specific standards
- Projected timelines or schedules
- Access to resources

When at work, at home, and in community situations, you need to know what is asked or required. If you do not know the specifics, you feel uncertain and are apt to spin your wheels, never sure if something is good enough. Lack of specifics about a task increases your avoidance of it, and makes you more vulnerable to procrastination or perfectionism.

This is especially true if the tasks are difficult, boring, or overwhelming: completing new job responsibilities, doing taxes, or filling out forms. In such situations, you may face serious consequences if the task isn't finished in a timely, accurate, and complete manner.

Another way assertive skills can help you is to reduce over commitment at work, at home, or in your community. Plan a response that lets you off the hook when someone requests that you take or extend a responsibility. You could say, "Thanks for asking. Under other circumstances, I would like to participate but I'm not able to at this time."

Schedule Tasks and Activities

The development of a realistic schedule helps you deal with multiple and often competing roles and responsibilities. When you are developing your schedule, try to keep a clear focus on your priorities and goals. This will reduce the chance that you get trapped in a life that doesn't reflect your truest values.

An effective schedule helps protect you from wasting time on nonessentials. You can impose some limits on activities you enjoy but that should be curbed, such as lengthy phone conversations.

Transferring items from your "to-do" list to a schedule helps you be more realistic in your planning. In addition, once the schedule has been written, it's easier to spot conflicts, monitor your behavior, and make changes as necessary.

Here are some tips to help you more effectively schedule your tasks and activities:

- Consider your personal style. If you're a slow-but-sure person, allow enough time in your schedule to think about, complete, and check over the tasks you perform.
- Schedule specific times for transitions and allow for unexpected delays such as traffic or poor weather conditions.
- Use your highest energy time for analytic or creative thought. For example, many people are less alert in the late afternoon.
- Use color coding when you write out a schedule. This reduces mistakes and is especially important if you are generating a family calendar, where different members have different activities.
- Use your schedule to help you say "no" to over commitment! For example, if you are running back-to-back with meetings and shouldn't try to fit in anything else, say, "I wish I could meet but it is impossible this week. Let me suggest an alternative."

Organize Tasks and Activities

In many offices and homes, systems are lacking for organizing and storing materials, equipment, or supplies. There isn't a process for accessing information or completing important activities such as how to record insurance payments or what to do if there is an accident. Although there are good intentions, no one "gets around to it." There are too many distractions.

The lack of organization results in needless clutter and messiness in the office or home. You waste time, are frustrated, and become increasingly distracted and stressed. Here are a few tips to cut down on the distraction that a mess creates:

- Consolidate errands by geographic location to save time and energy.
- Set small goals. Tackle one job at a time.
- Set a schedule for each goal and check each task as completed.
- Develop checklists to outline procedures, steps, and sequences.
- Store records in binders if you tend to lose or misplace papers and files.
- Monitor your efficiency. Should you maintain or revise your plan? Can some tasks be grouped together?

Distractions and Finance

The news is filled with stories about people who inadvertently drift into debt and financial insecurity. When you are constantly rushed, stressed, and/or fatigued, you may be distracted from carefully focusing on your finances. You may incur a variety of nasty costs and consequences including debt and distress. For example, you might:

- Assume that someone else is efficiently taking care of bills when they are not.
- Forget to deposit payments and overdraw your bank account.
- Fail to collect monies owed to you or your business.
- Incur needless, excessive interest payments or late fees, penalties, or fines.
- Fall prey to marketing hype and use too many credit cards.
- Be remiss in reviewing or catching errors in financial reports.

You can take some small steps to avoid such problems. For example, make a commitment and a contract with yourself (or other family members) to pay attention to basic financial matters. To defeat the subtle but pernicious effect of distractions upon your finances, try to:

- Plan and budget, especially before a holiday season or a special event such as a wedding.
- Use a debit rather than a credit card or use a cash/ checkbook system.
- Use an automated deposit and bill paying system.
- Set a time each week or month to pay bills, balance accounts, and review finances.
- Deal immediately with debt: set small goals, and prioritize which debts to pay off first. For example, say, "Pay utilities before department store accounts."
- Work with a trusted, nonjudgmental person to start getting a handle on your finances.
- Learn all you can about personal finance issues such as credit card accounts. For example, have you read the small print on a credit card application? Is the interest rate fixed or are you being lured by an introductory

teaser? Do you qualify for the advertised rate or is it for premium cards only? You may need to shop around.

- Stop yourself when you make statements that sabotage your efforts, such as, "Oh, it doesn't matter that much." or "I'll just pay it off next month."

If you need help in refocusing on your financial health, you may find support in a 12-step program such as Debtors Anonymous, *www.debtorsanonymous.org*, or through an accredited, nonprofit member of the National Foundation for Credit Counseling, *www.nfcc.org*.

Transitions from One Task to Another

Many of us aren't finished with one activity before we rush headlong into another. Rushing distracts us and presents barriers to full attention. Under these circumstances, we rarely feel that we've accomplished what we've set out to do, even if we have accomplished a lot.

You can reduce distractions and improve your attention by having a routine that ensures that you end one task before moving on to another.

Here are 10 steps to stop ineffective transitions and improve your effectiveness:

1. Identify a goal and time period(s) to work on a task.

2. Set a timer.

3. Take a break when the task is completed.

4. Review what has been accomplished at the end of the allotted time.

5. Check off parts that are completed and those that need additional time.

6. Continue work or stop and schedule additional work periods.

7. Congratulate yourself for adhering to a routine.

8. Take a breather—even if it is only for a minute or two.

9. Move to a different chair or location.

10. Begin this routine with another task.

Scheduled breaks, previews, and reviews help you focus more effectively when you are shifting from one activity or task to another. For example, many companies schedule back-to-back meetings, but the most efficient ones designate the final 15 minutes for the logistics of closing out the materials from one meeting, retrieving the materials needed for the next meeting, and moving between the two. At the end of the day, some working parents "take five" just before entering the hectic home/dinner setting. This provides a brief respite so they can quiet down from work.

Similarly, commuters take a few minutes to regroup before they move from the congestion of traffic to the pressures of their work situation. They may park at the farthest spot in the parking lot to ensure that they have a few minutes of walking and cooling off before entering their job site.

During the day, some people read the newspaper or listen to a song to help them warm up or shift from one activity to another. Whatever the technique, your attention will be enhanced by instituting a short routine to finish a task and taking a mini-break before beginning another activity.

Appropriate Multitasking

Dora is someone whose performance plummets when there is a 25% reduction in office staff. Originally hired to process insurance forms, Dora's desk was in the back part of the office where

*it's relatively quiet with few distractions. As the office staff has di-
minished, she's moved closer and closer to the reception area. First,
she's asked to answer the phone. Next, she's asked to "occasionally"
deal with clients.*

*As the months go by, Dora is increasingly required to be on
the phone with clients and other staff. When her speed and accuracy suffer, her supervisor becomes irritated and asks, "What's the
problem? This isn't the kind of performance that we need. What
am I going to write in your performance appraisal?"*

Dora has two problems. First, Dora is a person who works in a
slow but accurate manner. She requires a bit of effort to arouse
her attention. When she finally focuses, she is easily distracted.

Second, Dora's supervisor is unaware of ongoing research
about multitasking. Researchers Joshua Rubenstein, Ph.D., David
Meyer, Ph.D., and Jeffrey Evans, Ph.D. at the University of Michigan demonstrated that carrying on several duties at once may reduce productivity, not increase it. You would think that the
researchers were talking about Dora in their report. Interviewed
by CNN, Meyer states that "people in a work setting who are
banging away on word processors at the same time they have to
answer phones and talk to their co-workers or bosses—they're
doing switches all the time. Not being able to concentrate for, say,
tens of minutes at a time may mean it's costing a company as
much as 20 to 40 percent in terms of potential efficiency lost, or
the 'time cost' of switching. These 'time costs' increased with the
complexity of the chores: It took longer for subjects to switch between more complicated tasks." He compared the time cost
process as briefly having writer's block as you go from one task to
another (Anderson, 2001).

For better or for worse, multitasking is fast becoming a new
requirement for many in the workforce. Employers constantly expect their staff members to do more with less. Multitasking can

be an advantage when done well and a disadvantage when done poorly. It is a mistake, however, to assume that everyone can automatically adapt to new demands.

Effective multitasking requires applying many of the same principles we've already covered such as selecting a quiet time and place, breaking the work down into manageable chunks, taking breaks, and creating a feedback process.

In addition, consider the following 7 steps to ensure effective multitasking:

1. Understand and share the research about multitasking with those at work.

2. Consider the complexity of the task you are required to do.

3. Know your strengths and preferred style.

4. Know your limitations.

5. Be selective about where and when to do several things at once.

6. If you're inexperienced with a type of task or setting, check the period of time during which you can most effectively multitask.

7. If you're experienced, be on the lookout for times during which multitasking is ineffective.

Overcome Procrastination

We are vulnerable to distractions when a task is perceived as overwhelming, irrelevant, tedious, or difficult. Such tasks trigger an avoidance response. It's common to allow ourselves to be distracted by almost anything so we postpone beginning a task; we watch one more television program, make one more phone call, play one more video game, search for a snack, or play with a pet.

*With her manuscript finished and on the way to the publisher, Jo-
lene's study looks like a cyclone has hit it; papers, folders, books,
pamphlets, journals, markers, and index cards covering the desk
and much of the floor. She closes the door—for several days.
Clearing the clutter is the last thing she wants to do. She finished
the book—isn't that enough?*

    *She begins work on her new project in the kitchen, putting off
the need to clean up. She curses herself each time she needs something in her study since she can't readily find what she needs.*

Jolene devised the following plan to begin and complete a task
that she didn't want to do. She didn't permit her new project to
distract her from this arduous task. She decided to work on her
new project only after spending time clearing her study. Jolene's
plan reduced her vulnerability to distraction and procrastination.
She created inviting conditions and consequences to get her
started and keep her clearing the clutter.

    You might find these 9 steps useful:

1. Schedule several *clearing up* times of one to two hours.

2. Set an alarm clock to signal the end of *clearing up* time.

3. Use yarn or tape to divide the room into a grid of 8, 10,
   or 12 sections. Set a goal to clean a specific number of
   grids during each clear-up session.

4. Select an interesting audio book or music. Listen for 30
   minutes while you work and then take a short break.

5. Begin by clearing the easiest section.

6. Put a small piece of candy in each section. Enjoy the
   candy as each section is cleared.

7. Take a photo as each section is completed and tape it in a
   visible place.

8. Plan fun/relaxing activities to do during breaks.

9. Stop when the alarm rings. Review progress and congratulate yourself.

Avoid the "Haste Makes Waste" Syndrome

Rushing prevents you from paying attention to important cues and signals that are necessary to effectively complete a task or engage in an activity. When rushing, you may skip or reverse steps, follow the wrong sequence, or ruin the outcome of the activity.

Cathy's story:

It's 8:30 AM on a cold, windy morning in the parking lot of the Park City Ski Resort in Utah. Rushing to get four children, ages 4 to 12, out of the car and onto the slopes is no easy feat. I am the guardian of four sets of boots, gloves, hats, goggles, lip balms, gum, money, and neck warmers, plus a set for myself. Two kids are sleepy, another hungry, and the fourth, grouchy. My husband helps a lot by yelling, "Come on, we don't have all day. What's the problem? Let's go!" As I get myself ready, I also need to give my kids a last-minute safety talk.

Needless to say, I feel hassled, rushed, and cold. By 9:30 AM, the children are with ski instructors and my husband and I at the chairlift. Finally, the frenzy of the early morning has passed.

That first ride up the mountain is glorious. We ignore the wind and blowing snow and focus on each other and the sunshine. At 8,000 feet, we begin our first run. But something isn't right. Although we stick to intermediate runs, my feet begin to ache. By mid-mountain, I'm hurting. By the bottom, I'm in agony. In the middle of the second run, the pain from my new boots can no longer be ignored. I squat to wipe the deep snow from the front of them and to my surprise, my feet are pointing in different directions. My new boots didn't stand a chance, seeing as how I had put them on the wrong feet. That explains my agony.

In a business setting, rushing can cause embarrassment and a tarnished image greater than Cathy experienced.

Martin's story:

Martin, a consultant, arrives at his client's office, anticipating hot java. The secretary is out of the office that day, and given that the office has an informal atmosphere, Martin says he'll make the coffee. "No problem. I make the coffee every morning. I'm a star in the kitchen."

Martin zips into the small kitchen area, rushing so he won't lose important time with his client. He grabs the coffee pot parts from the drain board and practically throws the coffee into the paper filter while flying out to the meeting room. A bit later a team member leaves the meeting room and tells Martin she will bring him a cup of coffee. When she returns, however, she smiles but doesn't bring the coffee. Martin asks if everything is alright. She says, "It's fine. Just wait. I mean, forget about it."

Not one to let anything slip by, Martin excuses himself and goes into the kitchen. He is aghast to find coffee grounds and muddy liquid all over the floor, counter, and sink. To make things worse, one of the firm's partners is on her hands and knees cleaning it up. Not paying attention, he had failed to put the top on the pot and this mess was the result.

Cathy and Martin experienced distractions when rushing. For them, attention disconnections like this happen once in a while.

Too many of us, however, live a rushed life. Constantly being late robs us of energy and attention. We spill drinks, drop papers, forget directions, lose supplies, make careless mistakes, and feel overwhelmed and frustrated. The more rushed we are, the less attention is available to help us perform with efficiency.

Try these tips to slow down your rushed life:

- Be conscious of the negative effects of rushing on your accomplishment of necessary tasks and activities.
- Use a strategy such as Stop, Look, and Listen to pause, slow down, talk to yourself, and avert mishaps. (Refer to Chapter 2.)
- Think of your goals and priorities before you rush into a situation so you can avoid misjudgments and maintain your competent, professional image.
- Use tried and true time management techniques such as checklists and schedules to ensure that you have ample time to complete tasks and make transitions. Sometimes rescheduling an activity is the best option.
- Develop routines that keep you on time, such as using alarms on PDAs to keep you on time for meetings. You might want to have your PDA or watch signal the ending time of a meeting, shopping trip, or kid pick-up so you can be on time for the next activity.

For many people, the morning routine in particular causes problems that set the stage for a full day of distractions and mishaps. Here are 10 steps to improve the common problem of morning rush:

1. Keep a chart by the door that lists the equipment or supplies you need to take with you such as your cell phone, parking change or transit card, keys, wallet, water, or snacks.

2. Review your schedule the night before and assemble needed materials.

3. Pack the backpack, attaché case, and/or car the night before.

4. Ready the coffee pot and breakfast supplies the night before.

5. Set out clothes in advance.

6. Set clocks and watches ahead by 5 to 15 minutes.

7. Set one or two alarm clocks. The first provides a five- or ten-minute warning and the second provides the "Get out of the house NOW" signal.

8. Allot 5 to 15 minutes extra to leave in an orderly fashion for special events.

9. Get up 15 to 20 minutes earlier than usual.

10. Keep track of your progress. Congratulate yourself if you are progressing and readjust the routine if you are not.

Special Events: A Playground for the Demons

Whether joyous or tragic, everyday fun or a once-in-a-lifetime experience, special events create conditions that present unusual distractions *and* pose threats to safety and efficient performance.

You are at risk of making mistakes and omissions during activities that involve high emotional intensity: births, deaths, or celebrations. Distracted by add-on roles/responsibilities, you need to be especially vigilant during special life events so that mistakes are kept to a minimum.

Whenever special events are in the making, consider the following:

• Talk to experts related to the life events in which you are involved. For example, when moving, ask agents for checklists. Checklists and other resources, which are commonly provided by real estate, insurance, or health companies, can be extremely helpful.

• If finances allow, delegate the planning and management of special events such as weddings to professionals.

- Alert others to your increased level of stress, fatigue, and/or distractibility and enlist their support. For example, ask family members to put requests or information in written form such as e-mail instead of expecting you to remember extra details in your head.
- Usually, tragedies require a complete time-out from daily responsibilities. Rely on family, friends, and experts to take charge, attend to the details, and support you for some brief time until you get back on track.

Whether every day or on special occasions, you need to be mindful of how many tasks and activities you're taking on and how you are handling them.

DEMON BUSTERS: Employ Tactical Control over the Activities Demon

Beware and prepare. You can better guard against distractions and ensure effective performance when you:

✦ Identify activities that can make you vulnerable to distractions.

✦ Eliminate multitasking as much as you can.

✦ Establish transition routines to help you move from one task or activity to another.

✦ Recognize and allow for the extra distractions posed by special events.

✦ Take steps to prevent your procrastinating and rushing habits.

✦ Use assertive skills to end your habit of over scheduling.

The **Spaces Demon** lurks where we live, work, or play. Being distracted by sights and sounds or wallowing in messy, unpleasant settings leads to feeling overwhelmed, to inaccurate work, and to a slower pace.

6

Defeating the Spaces Demon

Do any of these things happen to you?

- *"The desk was really cluttered; photographs, correspondence, and flyers. I couldn't focus on the bills."*
- *"I couldn't find the file when the customer was waiting."*
- *"We were supposed to have a working lunch but the staff lounge was so noisy, I couldn't concentrate."*
- *"I've had to replace three cell phone chargers in the last six months. Every time I'm out of town, I feel unhinged and out of routine. Even when I check the room, I miss one thing or another."*
- *"My cubicle is near the lounge area where everyone congregates. All the action there is distracting. I know I shouldn't care, but I want to know what's going on."*

How similar are these conditions to those you confront each day?

The conditions within the physical spaces where we work, live, and socialize can distract us to the point that we make mistakes, procrastinate, or forget things. Common distracting places and spaces include restaurants, airports, kitchens, and work cubicles.

Throughout the day (and night), we are bombarded by stimuli that distract us and disrupt our attention. It's time to examine the conditions in the places where we work or play and discover how to minimize distractions so we can maximize our focus. This chapter helps you defend against distractions when in cubicles, shared office spaces, and public areas. You'll find some suggestions on how to meet the increasing challenges posed by travel.

Distractions in the Cubicle Culture

Victor, a high-powered researcher in a manufacturing company, doesn't complete his reports.

Because his work is highly technical, Victor needs to concentrate to ensure its accuracy. When he gets to the office early, no one else is there so he can have quiet time to work. But as soon as the morning shift shows up, chaos reigns.

In his work environment, Victor feels overwhelmed by the constant ringing of land and cell phones, noise from the fax machines, bits and pieces of conversation, and people passing by. In addition, he is near a window and can get distracted by outside sights and sounds.

Unaware of Victor's challenges, his supervisor gets irritated at him. "He's always here. Why can't he get the reports done on time?" he asks.

Almost 70 percent of today's office workers do not have private offices according to a survey conducted by the American Society of Interior Designers in 2005. Although many designers have praised the usefulness of cubicles, evidence indicates that they offer little protection against distractions (Veitch, Charles, and Newsham, 2004).

If you experience chaos like Victor does, how can you reduce distractions caused by the Spaces Demon, and complete your work more quickly?

Reduce Environmental Disruptions

Start by changing various elements in your work setting. Here are some suggestions:

- Put up a "Do Not Disturb" sign or picture of a clock with moveable hands to indicate when you are available. Let people know that you are unavailable at certain work times.
- Post a general message such as "I'm on the phone or otherwise unavailable. Please leave a message including your phone number and e-mail address," or "I return calls within ___ minutes (hours) or during the following hours ___."
- Institute an electronic lockdown in your office area: no phone, television, beepers, and so forth.
- Lower the ringer so you don't even hear the phone and let the answering machine record messages.
- Don't disturb or distract others by striking up a conversation when they're concentrating.

Reduce Visual Distractions

- Sit facing a wall.
- Make a cardboard screen or, if allowed, wear a hat or visor to block out distractions.
- Remove distracting signs or posters.

- Clear a spot on a messy desk or cover a messy table with a heavy cloth.

Reduce Auditory Distractions

- Use earplugs to screen out noise.
- Close the door and/or window.
- Use a fan or other mechanical device to provide white noise or purchase a noise reduction device such as Sound Screen.
- Use your own voice to screen out other sounds by talking or whispering instructions to yourself about how to most productively do the task in which you are engaged.
- Use background music or peaceful nature sounds to screen out other distracting sounds.

Access Resources

- Work at a different desk or table in a secluded or quiet area such as a library.
- Talk to your supervisor, describe what you plan to do, and ask for suggestions to support your need.

Institute a Modified Open-Door Policy

Must you be available to everyone, all the time?

The answer is "yes" at one insurance company headquartered in Boston. When a consultant asked if it was permissible to close the door to allow better "think time," the manager said, "No, how can we make sure people are really working if the door is closed?"

If you're obliged to have an open-door policy but can't think due to interruptions, consider moving the door to a less open position for a portion of the day. Discuss having a group "high performance think time" at a certain time during the day or week. If you run into crises all day, perhaps an upgrade of policies, work processes, or job aids can reduce the need to engage in constant problem solving.

Deal with Clutter in a Shared Work Space

Here's how Alice, a laboratory technologist, uses her assertiveness skills to reduce distractions in the work space she shares with Ed.

Alice works the evening shift in a small cubicle in a large, open, clinical laboratory. Ed works the early shift. Alice is neat as a pin and very detailed-oriented. Ed is not. Although Ed likes his work, he often finds the procedures tedious. He works hard to maintain his focus and concentration. He engages in a number of activities to keep him alert such as eating candy, chewing gum, drinking coffee, and wadding up scrap papers to play basketball around the cubicle. His cubicle is a mess when he leaves at the end of his shift.

Every night, Alice gets aggravated and distracted because her work space is cluttered with used clinical supplies, dirty coffee cups, and wads of paper. On several occasions, she has grasped the countertop to push her chair closer to the desk and found used gum stuck to her fingers—a sign of Ed's inattentiveness.

Alice decides to talk to Ed directly instead of having conversations with him in her head and feeling stressed about it. She believes she has a right to a clean work space and to conditions that help rather than hinder her attention and work performance.

So the next morning, Alice calls Ed and says, "Ed, can you help me out? I can't concentrate when our cubicle is messy. It may not seem like a big deal but it is not pleasant to begin a new shift with old supplies and gum wrappers. Could you take a minute or two before you leave to straighten up? I'd really appreciate it."

This assertive approach did not attack Ed; it merely stated Alice's needs with a clear request for change.

Alice could have spoken to her supervisor and would have if Ed's reactions to her request had been negative or explosive. In this case, however, she decided that she could use her assertive skills to get cooperative behavior from her co-worker. As a result, she felt she had greater control and confidence when handling the issues she found distracting.

Ed, an easygoing person, apologized for the mess he created and pledged to do a better job. Alice thanked him for his efforts and, although he slipped periodically, she gained a work environment that enhanced her ability to concentrate.

You can help gain better attention connections at work and at home by letting people know about your needs and wants.

Remember, you can do the following:

- Just say "no" (politely) when others ask if they can interrupt you.
- Alert people to the times you're unavailable and can't be interrupted.
- Use a "Do Not Disturb Sign" or a smiling face with the words "Quiet, Genius at Work."
- Establish regularly scheduled work/think periods alone and with others.
- Keep group members on track and prevent distractions by having an agenda and timetable.
- Alert others to the style by which you learn best and pay attention to the styles used by others in your office.

- Ask for your co-workers' cooperation when it's especially important to pay full attention.

Assertiveness in Public Spaces and Places

If you get distracted by sights or sounds or you're hard of hearing, then avoid noisy, busy, and visually cluttered places. Your assertiveness skills can help you avoid distractions and create conditions for better communication.

For example, if someone wants to eat at a crowded, noisy place, you have choices and can make suggestions like these:

"Let's go to a different restaurant; the tables are crowded too close together."

"Let's sit away from the window, toward the back."

"Let's limit the number of people to four or six."

"I'm going to ask the hostess to lower the volume on the music."

Travel Troubles

Bob, a speaker and trainer, travels to various cities. The more he travels, the more money he makes. The more he travels, however, the crazier he feels. He misplaces tickets, chargers, and directions, packs mismatched outfits, and can't keep track of expenses. On his latest trip, he goes to the wrong hotel and is charged a full night's fee by not showing up at the place where he'd made a reservation. That is money down the drain.

Bob, like so many who must travel for business, can benefit from using simple travel-related aids to plan his trips and keep him on track.

At the beginning, ask yourself:

- What do I need to pack?
- Where am I going and how am I getting there?
- What equipment, materials, or supplies must I bring?
- How can I keep on track and not misplace items when traveling?

We feel comfortable in our homes because we can locate the possessions, predict the noises, appreciate the conveniences, and know how much time is needed to travel from place to place. Our routines get thrown out of whack when we travel.

It's natural to become distracted and leave or lose important documents at busy airports. The solution? Wear a travel pouch around your neck or waist and put in it your tickets, identification, directions, tip money, and so on.

Especially in these days of high security, air travel requires thinking ahead. Do you allot enough time to deal with possible check-in and security problems? Do you leave behind excessive jewelry, belts, and cumbersome shoes? Rule of thumb: the fewer things you carry, the less you'll worry about or be distracted by.

Be sure to expect the unexpected and accept that travel will increase your vulnerability to attention disconnections. Look out for possible pitfalls that can occur when you feel rushed, tired, and tense or in an unfamiliar environment.

Go for a preemptive strike and follow these 10 suggestions for reducing travel hassle:

1. Make a copy of your driver's license, passport, credit cards, and airline ticket receipt. Carry the copies in a separate folder or case. Do not bring Social Security or Medicare cards. This makes you less vulnerable to identity theft.

2. Make a list of your medications and dosage for each one, and place the vials in a see-through plastic bag for easier

screening at airport security. Take an extra day's supply with you in case your return is delayed.

3. Keep repeating to yourself, or write a note on your boarding pass, about the number of items going through the security belt in bins. In case you must be individually checked, make sure that your computer and/or cell phone is not hidden if security personnel put one bin on top of another. Don't be one of the hundreds of passengers paged to return to security to retrieve your cell phone!

4. Have a special place such as an attaché case, envelope, or drawer to keep hotel-based parking ticket, room key, car keys, and business cards, so you aren't always looking for them. Also, don't forget to use an envelope, plastic bag, or wallet to hold your home parking lot ticket, taxi telephone number, or pick-up reservation number so you can get home easily.

5. Take a pocket map or write directions if you go walking in unfamiliar neighborhoods. (Don't do what I did. One morning in Paris I took a walk, but didn't take the hotel card or my purse. As a result, I wandered around for an hour asking for directions back to the hotel in my pidgin French. Finally, a policeman showed me the way back.)

6. Complete a travel expense form or list expenses in your PDA during the trip so you don't have to do it when you get home.

7. Make a checklist of items you're taking from home and use this to make sure you have packed everything before leaving your hotel room.

8. Post a note on the door to remind yourself to pick up items commonly left behind such as a telephone charger, tape recorder, PDA, connecting cables, and so forth.

9. Pack a small bag of supplies including transparent tape and a sewing kit.

10. Pay special attention to the shower/tub fixture where you're staying. Dealing with unfamiliar fixtures, you could end up showering your hair when you meant to fill the tub.

Working on the Road

Carlos is a management consultant who's always on the run, driving from city to city and event to event. He's grateful that business is good but feels frantic because he's always rushing and neglecting to put things away. Annual reports, surveys, and references are stuffed into his case and, on occasion, disappear. Once he gets home, he drops his bags and begins getting ready for the next trip.

Creating structure and routine is critical when you work on the road. Following these 10 tips is highly recommended:

1. Create an office/data management system that's accessible while traveling. Use it to file information about clients or input information about projects.

2. Fill out expense account information daily and use folders or envelopes to store receipts in your car or briefcase.

3. Keep equipment and accessories in labeled plastic bags. Create and maintain a checklist of items to refer to before leaving a site.

4. Use a flash memory device for your computer to archive all your presentations.

5. Bring with you a formatted client data sheet to record pertinent information if you're doing any marketing on the road.

6. Keep a map, first aid kit, emergency road kit, extra per-

sonal items, batteries and other supplies, and healthy snacks in your car.

7. Schedule monthly maintenance for your car.

8. Plan your driving route using maps or GPS system.

9. Make an extra set of keys and attach them to the underside of your car.

10. Plan on taking at least 30 minutes to put things away, file papers, or replenish supplies after each trip. Give yourself these instructions and follow them: "I have to finish one thing before I start another!"

Yes, you *can* be more mindful of the positive conditions that contribute to your effectiveness in the places and spaces in which you work or play.

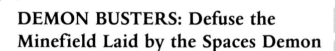

DEMON BUSTERS: Defuse the Minefield Laid by the Spaces Demon

To ensure high performance and reduce the sights and sounds that distract you, be sure to:

✦ Assume responsibility for reducing distractions.

✦ Actively rearrange the settings in which you operate.

✦ Alert others to your need for uninterrupted and distraction-free time to get things done.

The **STRESS DEMON** can be activated by internal or external triggers, robbing us of the psychic energy needed to pay attention. Without conscious attention to stress management, we make too many mistakes.

7

Defeating the Stress Demon

Paula's son, Tony, is in surgery to remove a brain tumor. While her daughter-in-law stays at the hospital, Paula drives the older grandchild to school and then returns with the infant and toddler to wait for the babysitter. When the babysitter arrives, she looks with concern at Paula and says, "Hi, are you OK?" Paula replies, "Sure. I'm doing just fine." The babysitter laughs and says, "Well, did you mean to leave your purse next to the car in the middle of the driveway and the keys in the door?"

Many of us have such stories. We think that we are doing just fine but our performance slips. We forget things, make errors, and lack energy for tedious tasks. The stress of another's illness may not be apparent to us but it distracts us. It is during such times that we need to be especially watchful about taking care of our personal things (e.g., keys, glasses, wallets) and following safety guidelines like wearing safety belts.

When the Stress Demon attacks, we are more vulnerable to mix-ups and accidents.

This chapter identifies common types and sources of stress, how stress acts as a distraction, and how to better manage stress in your life so that you can be productive in spite of it.

Stress as a Distraction

"Stressed is DESSERTS spelled backward." This phrase has been written on a poster and greeting card. Yes, one common result of stress is the craving for sweets or comfort foods, but another result of stress is inattention.

Stress is a demon that interferes with your ability to tap into your attention reservoir. You attempt to pay attention and your innards groan, your mind wanders, and you just can't go on. Or, you begin to pay attention but make errors and are blocked from creative thoughts. Stress drains your attention. As a result, you lose efficiency and effectiveness. In other words, you lose your edge at work or suffer adverse effects on your health.

Types of Stress

All stress is not alike. It is easy to see that some stress is more intense or long-term than others.

According to a report by The Stress Knowledge Company (2000), stress can be classified into four different types:

1. Acute stress.

With this kind of stress, you might experience agitation, moodiness, irritability, headaches, and/or gastrointestinal upset. Stress busters usually reduce this type of difficulty if you are both mindful and proactive.

2. Episodic acute stress.

This kind of stress is more significant and can lead to migraines, high blood pressure, emotional difficulties, and serious gastrointestinal distress. It usually requires long-term changes in lifestyle and professional help.

3. Chronic stress.

Chronic stress is very serious because it makes us vulnerable to systemic illnesses. It compromises our immune system and although it can be reversed, it usually takes time and professional intervention.

4. Traumatic stress.

Traumatic stress may follow personal or other tragedies. Posttraumatic stress disorder has been in the news as a result of events like 9/11, Hurricane Katrina, and foreign wars. Less discussed are the personal effects of sudden job loss, death of a loved one, violent attack, or abuse. Such events should be addressed with the aid of a professional.

Although most stress is treatable, the type and length of intervention depends on the degree of stress experienced and how long-standing it is.

Helena works as a housekeeper during the day and lives with an abusive, alcoholic husband at night. She tries to be an empathetic and understanding wife as she lives with the situation. When her husband's problems deepen and his outbursts become more frequent, she becomes increasingly more concerned about the safety of herself and her son. She begins to have symptoms of irritable bowel syndrome. On the job, she drops or breaks things. She becomes short-tempered with her son. When she visits her doctor to deal with her increasingly severe gastrointestinal problems, her physician suggests medication, counseling, and a stress

management program. She comments to her doctor, "I didn't real-
ize the ways that stress was piling up and making me sick."

In Helena's case, it takes a slow buildup of physical symptoms
and a visit to a physician before she even considers the stress-
mind-body connection.

Common Causes of Stress

Life is complicated; financial pressures and poor working conditions are just two conditions that contribute to general tension.
For example, 40% of workers reported their job was very or extremely stressful while 25% view their jobs as the number one
stressor in their lives. These conditions within our environments
are beyond our control and contribute to uncertainty. Against this
background, we can face personal difficulties that can trigger
stress.

Some individuals cope more easily than others. They seem
more resilient and continue to pay attention even when under
stress. Even these people, however, may become so stressed that
their attention suffers. For example, although Paula usually copes
well with stress, the serious nature of her son's surgery triggers a
different type and level of stress that leads to attention slippages.
They not only surprise her; they can endanger her grandchildren.

Such reactions may also occur when a series of seemingly
minor upsets, each of which alone could be coped with easily,
occur within a short time.

Many people do not realize how pervasive stress becomes
during major life changes. They don't plan ample rest or relaxation during these times.

Often, a person, family, or business simultaneously faces several major changes. During these times, stress should be considered a major distraction that needs to be dealt with.

Some of the common causes of major stress include:

- Death of a loved one
- Onset of an illness, disease, or chronic condition
- Serious illness or accident of a significant other or family member
- Departure of a partner, lover, or friend
- Change or loss of a job
- Moving to a new home or place of business
- Home or business reconstruction projects
- Financial setback or personal or career failure
- Change in status with a spouse or significant other
- Introduction of a child into one's life through pregnancy, birth, adoption, or remarriage

Keep a Stress Diary

Knowing the enemy is half the battle. Writing about your stress in a diary will help you develop greater insight.

To keep a stress awareness diary for a week or two, make a note of the day and time a stressful event occurs. Review the event in your mind and identify the physical or emotional stress symptom you experienced (e.g., inability to concentrate, headache, tightness in neck, irritability, restlessness, etc.).

Note what triggered the stress and what happened afterward. Reflect on when and for how long you felt stressed during a day or week. Looking at the bigger picture—how vulnerable are you to stress? How chronic is it? Then review how the stress affected your ability to pay attention to important tasks or events in your life. Write it all down.

General Strategies to Deal with the Stress Demon

Some stress is unavoidable. Some stress helps to focus attention. Too much stress, however, overwhelms and affects our health and welfare and detracts our attention from our work and relationships.

Consider deploying these 8 strategies for resisting the Stress Demon.

1. Check your sleep/fatigue and other health factors. You need both physical and mental strength to deal with stressful events.

2. Don't ignore physical symptoms of stress such as headaches, sleeplessness, nervous stomach, or the jitters.

3. Identify your top three methods of handling stress and use them.

4. Check the amount of caffeine, nicotine, and alcohol you consume. Each may provide some short-term relief from stress but can have long-term negative effects on your mood and sleep patterns.

5. Find some new techniques to provide temporary relief of stress. For example, use humor to relax prior to beginning tasks that are boring, difficult, or require prolonged attention.

6. Don't ignore frequent comments from others such as, "Is something bothering you?" "Why are you so irritable?" or "You seem really stressed-out."

7. Check with a mental health professional. Discuss your stress symptoms as they relate to your stage of life, physical health, or life circumstances.

8. Develop a support system and/or social network. Studies have shown how the increase of social support can greatly reduce stress levels.

Everyday Stress Busters

To minimize the effects of stress, assemble a set of tactics that you can employ every day. These are your personal stress busters.

Sure, *little* stresses can be expected but, unfortunately, too many at once may have a *big* stress effect.

Consider the stress triggered by nasty remarks from a boss, getting a flat tire, confronting a broken promise, disciplining bratty kids, cajoling a cranky spouse, or just putting up with rain! Each incident may not be *big* but, when combined, they can build into a major stress reaction by the end of the day.

Experiment with these stress busters:

- Breathe deeply. Take four to six deep breaths to a count of four.
- Take a break for five minutes at least every two hours.
- Go on a mental vacation. Imagine yourself in a relaxing situation or look at photographs of a vacation paradise.
- Appreciate nature; go out for fresh air and sunshine.
- Listen, sing, or dance to upbeat, spiritual, or classical music.
- Find something humorous to listen to, read, or do.
- Have a healthy snack such as flavored ice water, herbal tea, a granola bar, or gum.
- Take a stretch break or brisk walk; climb a few flights of steps.
- Write about your feelings in a journal or on scratch

paper. Even writing key words or making a sketch can relieve tension.

- Amuse yourself with a puzzle, yoyo, or Game Boy.
- Play with a pet or watch fish swim around an aquarium.
- Share a joke with a friend by phone or e-mail.

Do activities that appeal to your spirit and your senses:

- Meditate.
- Take a bubble bath or warm shower.
- Light scented candles.
- Eat delicious fruit, healthy sweets, or a variety of nuts.
- Use aromatic spices in your food and/or your environment.
- Snuggle in a soft blanket.
- Surround yourself with bright colors.
- Look at or buy fresh flowers.
- Get a foot, face, or body massage.
- Sit in a rocker, lounge, or massage chair.

Lifestyle Stress Management Strategies

Effective use of stress management strategies provides a greater sense of control, security, and predictability. It will help you feel less stressed and less fatigued. There are a variety of approaches that deal with the mind-body connection. These include: exercise, massage therapy, relaxation, mindfulness training, T'ai Chi, Yoga, and meditation.

Any of these are healthy ways to integrate stress management into your lifestyle. Whether any of these activities will help you deal with stress is difficult to predict. But be open-minded about them; the effectiveness of these approaches to reduce stress is supported by research (Patel, 2001).

Exercise is promoted as a healthy and inexpensive method of staying fit. People, however, commonly fail to work out. Have you heard these common excuses for not exercising? Do you make them, too?

"I don't have time."

"I don't see the benefit."

"I'm too tired."

There is a large quantity of evidence dealing with the mind-body connection that illustrates the effectiveness of exercise in improving mental well-being. This is accomplished largely through improved mood and self-perceptions (Fox, 2004).

In addition to other health benefits, exercise reduces stress, and should be integrated into your lifestyle. It's recommended you walk, jog, bicycle, or engage in an aerobic exercise for 20 to 30 minutes three to four times a week.

Massage therapy has long been recognized as a complementary approach to treating neck and back pain, muscle tightness, and fatigue. Massage improves circulation, which aids in recovery of muscle soreness. It helps your muscles relax and increases your endorphin levels.

Relaxation is an effective self-help method of dealing with stress. Over three decades ago, Herbert Benson, M.D., a faculty member at Harvard Medical School, wrote a book titled *The Relaxation Response* (1975, 2000). This book offers research-based strategies for relaxing the body by focusing one's mind. Dr. Benson determined that two components are required to produce the relaxation response: (1) a mental device such as a sound, word, phrase, or prayer repeated silently or aloud, and (2) a fixed gaze at an object. For some, reading a book to learn how to relax provides a good basis for experimentation and change. For others, an audio-tape is a great resource. If you'd prefer a more personalized or in-teractive approach, look for hospital or community center courses on stress relief for everyday living as well as for chronic pain or illness.

Mindfulness training focuses on cultivating inner resources to calm the mind and gain a perspective on life's difficulties. Ex-perts indicate that people can learn to consciously manage stress-ful situations in their daily lives. Several types of interventions are available and are called mindfulness-based cognitive therapy. These methods are increasingly offered in mental health and medical settings (Hayes, Follette, and Linehan, 2004).

T'ai Chi is an ancient moving meditation that uses a variety of postures and transitions to stretch and contract the muscles in the body. Its practice is based on the belief that if you can train yourself to focus on the present instead of dwelling on the past or the future, you will be better able to deal with reality by accept-ing it.

Yoga is a Hindu discipline for uniting the self with the supreme spirit through various stretching exercises, positions, and breathing. Yoga means 'yoking' of self through spiritual discipline and training. It places a strong emphasis on balance on all levels (Budilovsky, Adamson, and Flynn, 2006). With many forms of yoga readily available, you can check for resources in your com-munity or on the Internet.

Meditation is the process of observing the body and the mind intentionally, of letting your experience unfold from mo-ment to moment and accepting it as it is. The process typically involves sitting in silence for 10 to 40 minutes a day and ac-tively yet effortlessly directing the mind to a single point of focus such as the breath, a word (called a mantra), or an image. You can search the Internet for Web sites that provide information and tips (e.g., *www.mindandlife.org; www.mindfulnesstapes.com; www.zenguide.com*).

Yoga and meditation have been practiced for thousands of years. Today, it's estimated that 16.5 million American adults practice yoga while 15 million practice meditation.

Take Action

Sometimes you need to deal with stress head-on, as when intrusive thoughts insist on pulling your concentration away from all of the tasks at hand. One method of reducing the negative effects of intrusive thoughts is to limit the time you deal with them. Another method is to switch gears to more positive thoughts by identifying the things in life for which you are grateful.

Take Worry Breaks

If you just can't say "no" to worrying, then schedule breaks specifically to do just that: worry. Set aside a brief time and place to actively think about the issues or uncertainties and begin the problem-solving process. This allows you to experience a degree of relief and then access the energy you need to pay attention to your other responsibilities.

Here are 9 steps to help you benefit from your worry break:

1. Sit in a comfortable chair at a table or desk. This is your worry chair.

2. Take a piece of paper and write, scribble, or draw details about your worries. You can also type into the computer or talk into an audio recorder.

3. Identify and circle the items of worry you can do something about.

4. Spend five to ten minutes doing this.

5. Allow yourself only 5 to 10 minutes each hour to actively think about your worries.

6. Stretch, take a few deep breaths, and imagine yourself paying attention and working productively.

7. Congratulate yourself for completing your worry break and leave the chair.

8. Sit in a different chair for 40 or 50 minutes and see how you can better pay attention to your tasks in a productive way.

9. If an intrusive thought enters your mind, remind yourself that you've spent an appropriate time worrying for this hour and you'll return to worrying after your scheduled work time is over. For example, say: "Stop, it's useless to keep thinking about this now."

Repeat these steps several times during the day if necessary. However, if you find that you're not getting any relief from your worry breaks or other stress management strategies, perhaps it's time to seek the support of a friend or professional.

Take "Count Your Blessings" Breaks

There is ample evidence about the usefulness of focusing on the positives in your life (Seligman, 2002). Following the ideas of Positive Psychology, you focus on your strengths rather than weaknesses. You benefit from using the traits you already possess—including kindness, originality, humor, optimism, and generosity. Using your strengths helps you develop natural buffers against difficulties and their associated negative emotions.

In addition, other researchers report that focusing on the things for which you are grateful can help you experience more energy and optimism and less stress. You can apply this concept by counting your blessings. Remember the good things in life by jotting entries in a *gratefulness diary* or by contributing notes, photos or mementos to a *gratefulness jar*.

Schedule a few minutes each day (or week) to remember, visualize, and write about the things for which you are grateful. You may already do this when you place photos and mementos on refrigerator doors or desks, but these items can act as more than mere souvenirs. When stress attacks, schedule a brief gratefulness break. Consciously look at these items and think about the positives that they represent—a review of your blessings can help you move away from stressful thoughts. A random note on the Internet says it all: *Get an attitude of gratitude.*

Create Stress-Free Zones

Action speaks louder than words. If you want to reduce stress and decrease distractions that interfere with your performance, then rearrange the conditions and consequences in at least one part of your work/life. Start small. Visualize the times when you are not stressed, and brainstorm ways you can create more positive conditions during your day.

Carl, a public speaker, works out of an office in his home where he's constantly interrupted by various family members fighting. On a daily basis, he has to deal with marketing, phone calls, mail deliveries, and billing. He realizes that the stress from others in his envi-

ronment interferes with his concentration when he needs to develop a new presentation.

So Carl decides to create a Stress-Free Zone by arranging to work in a quiet room at the public library. He brings his laptop computer, a seat cushion, an evergreen aerosol, a mini fan, and healthy snacks. He shuts off his cell phone and sits with his back facing the door's window.

Before he begins work, he stretches, breathes deeply, and visualizes himself presenting his successful speech. During his session in his Stress-Free Zone, he's able to set attainable goals and take frequent breaks. He develops the new seminar in half the time it would take him if he was in his home office.

Carl identified when and where stress was disrupting his attention, concentration, and creativity. He arranged better conditions for one part of his work life. And you can, too.

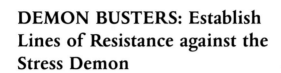

DEMON BUSTERS: Establish Lines of Resistance against the Stress Demon

Because stress is such an insidious, pervasive, and invasive factor in today's society, be sure to:

✦ Become aware of how stress diverts your attention and affects your physical and mental health.

✦ Increase your awareness of how stress undermines your attention and performance.

✦ Find ways (noted in this chapter) to avoid or disarm the negative effects of the Stress Demon.

✦ Make a commitment to regularly use simple techniques that will reduce and/or manage the stress you feel.

The *FATIGUE DEMON* saps the energy needed to focus and maintain concentration. Though we try to deny it, exhaustion leaves us spinning our wheels, committing errors, or even causing accidents.

8

Defeating the Fatigue Demon

Have you heard of these things happening?

- *An executive "zones out" at the wheel of his car, narrowly missing a school bus as he swerves across the median.*

- *A dentist nods off and snores periodically during a concert, interrupting the attention of others in the audience.*

- *A bank teller is tired and inattentive. As a result, customers get shortchanged and deposit slips get lost.*

These examples illustrate how the fatigue demon can present barriers to performance and foster unnecessary difficulties, even disasters, in our lives. For example, driving when fatigued, we may rush to work, ignore speed limits, and/or be vulnerable to road rage.

Additionally, our reaction time slows down when we feel tired. According to the National Highway Traffic Safety Administration, sleep-related automobile accidents kill over 1,500 people each year in the United States and cause more than 40,000 injuries (NHTSA, 2006).

This chapter examines the effects of fatigue on us as individuals and as a society. You'll discover routines to help fight fatigue and reduce your vulnerability to distraction.

The Fatigue Demon

The more fatigue you experience, the more vulnerable you are to distractions.

Few of us can escape the effects of fatigue on our attention and our ability to perform at peak levels—even the highest of achievers. For example, in an article entitled "An Excess of Foot-in-Mouth is Linked to a Lack of Shut-Eye," political candidates on the never ending campaign trail are reported to have increased irritability, verbal blunders, and hoarse voices (Cardwell, 2004).

Regardless of the type of work you do, chronic lack of sleep can hasten the onset or increase the severity of a number of other health problems, including diabetes, high blood pressure, and obesity.

When fatigue interferes with attention, there is a greater probability of the following:

- increased errors and failure to notice important details
- increased irritability and impatience
- feelings of stress and being overwhelmed
- reduced productivity
- decreased satisfaction with daily life

It's only when you're totally exhausted that you stop doing something because you can no longer focus or concentrate. Unfortunately, work done under such conditions often is inferior and has to be redone. As a result, you may work twice as long with only half the desired results.

The Impact of Fatigue in the Workplace

Consider the picture painted by a National Sleep Foundation survey by E. O. Johnson (2000): at least 43% of Americans say they are so sleepy that it interferes with their daily activities including work. Over 25% of employees are losing one third or more of their workweek to daytime sleepiness. The majority of them recognize that on-the-job drowsiness reduces the amount of work they complete, increases their frequency of errors, and hampers their decision-making and problem-solving abilities. Employees estimate that the quality and quantity of their work diminishes about 30% due to sleepiness.

On a national level, fatigue due to sleeplessness is costly. It is estimated that sleep deprivation costs $150 *billion* each year in higher stress and reduced worker productivity.

How Tired Are You?

Are you like many of your fellow Americans who report that they do not get the sleep they need? Over 80% report losing at least one hour of sleep a week—often, it's more like 5–8 hours. Have you actually fallen asleep on the job? One fourth of the adults surveyed by Shopzilla, Inc. admitted that they have (MSN Money, 2006)!

It is one thing to be tired from one or two late or sleepless nights. It's quite another to have sleeplessness and fatigue as part of your life pattern. Shortchanging your rest can hurt your health. Do you regularly get the amount of sleep experts recommend—7–8 hours a night?

About Bad Dreams and Nightmares

Timmy, a two-year-old, sprays some liquid from a red plastic bottle, its label reading "Monster Juice." He creeps and crawls around his room to all of the nooks and crannies he can find. He is careful not to miss any area under his bunk bed.

Queried about his intentions and actions, he replies, "I'm
spraying with Monster Juice, so they can't get me when I'm sleep-
ing. It really works!"

This unique and successful strategy helps this toddler cope with
the fears and nightmares he experiences as part of his normal
growth and development.

What about us? How often should we experience bad dreams
or nightmares? To what degree should we expect them as a part
of the normal adult experience? Are we battling demons while we
sleep? How restful and restorative is our sleep?

There are important reasons for dealing with frightening
dreams and fitful sleep. First, fitful sleep at night contributes to
fatigue during the day. Second, over the long term, fatigue increases our vulnerability to stress. Third, fatigue and stress make it
more difficult to pay attention. Last, when our attention wanders,
our performance falters.

If we have too many frightening dreams—or nightmares—
then we need to deal with such occurrences as a possible barrier
to positive attention and performance.

9 Techniques to Defeat the Fatigue Demon

1. Use a journal to list times you went to sleep, how long and
   how well you slept, and how you functioned the following day. Do this for a week or two.

2. View sleeplessness or sleep disturbances that cause fatigue
   as a barrier to attention that leads to performance problems. These problems won't be resolved without conscious
   thought and a plan of action.

3. Give yourself permission to change your sleep or rest routines. You could say, "I'm tired. It's all right to stop work-

ing and go to bed. I'll do a better job tomorrow when I'm more alert."

4. Plan to perform tasks requiring the highest levels of attention when you're most alert.

5. Take naps. They restore short-term alertness and enhance concentration and memory. Even napping for 10 minutes can refresh you.

6. Take short, frequent breaks, especially when performing tedious or boring tasks that require high speed and accuracy.

7. Take brief walks or stretch breaks before beginning a new activity.

8. Check your fatigue level before beginning a task and at regular intervals if your task requires sustained attention.

9. Reach out to your physician, media resources, friends, family, or possibly even hospital sleep clinics or research-based behavior therapy programs offered by psychologists. Your goal is to learn solutions about fatigue problems, particularly if you're experiencing chronic insomnia, bad dreams, nightmares, or "night terrors." Even one visit can shed light on the difficulty and lead to a positive resolution to the situation.

Getting Up and Going to Sleep Routines

Routines help you better connect your intention to action. It is tough to break the habit of going back to sleep after the alarm rings or staying up too late surfing the Internet.

Try these strategies to beat the Fatigue Demon.

Combat the "Oh How I Hate To Get Up In the Morning!" Syndrome

- Use an alarm that is placed away from the bed so you have to get up and turn it off.
- Find an alarm that keeps ringing and has a loud and irritating sound.
- Keep juice or a thermos of coffee by your bed.
- Get up as soon as you can after you awake. It reduces any negative feelings associated with too much sleep or staying in bed too long.
- Arrange your schedule to best reflect your natural or optimal sleep cycle, whenever possible.
- Ask others to telephone you and call back if you don't answer. (Place the telephone ringer on the highest volume so you'll hear it.)
- Use a lamp set on a timer to imitate the emergence of natural daylight or a light box to provide artificial sunlight. Such devices can brighten the start of the day.

Create a "Lullaby and Goodnight" Routine

- Avoid overstimulating activities immediately before bed including video games, arguing, and exercise. If you have an active imagination, this might also include reading and television.
- Introduce low-stimulus activities to cool down and relax, starting up to an hour before bedtime. This might include listening to soothing, instrumental music.
- Experiment with different relaxing activities and identify the ones that are most effective for you, given the time and situation.
- Create a nighttime routine including a consistent time

to go to bed. The routine might include listening to relaxing music or audiobooks.

- Identify your sleep-related creature comforts and gather
  them around you. Items might include: soft pillows,
  downy comforter, body-size sleep pillow, stuffed animal, or flannel sheets or pajamas.
- Set an alarm clock (or possibly two alarm clocks in different locations) to signal an end to non-sleep-related
  activities such as computer or video games.
- Use a lamp with a dimmer that gradually decreases
  light from full brightness to full dark in 45 minutes.
- Take a hot, soothing, pleasantly scented bath before
  bed.

Naps: A Shield against Fatigue

*Walter, a sales rep, must present the benefits of a newly developed
medical device to prospective buyers. His company provides a
basic format, but he must customize the presentation to the particular medical practice for which he is consulting. He's been told to
make the presentation crisp, interesting, accurate, and appropri-
ately detailed. He arrives home after putting in a 12-hour day.
After a quick bite to eat, he decides to tackle this task. His mind is
not responding.*

Should he nap for 20 or 30 minutes and then work for the hours it
takes to complete the presentation? Should he exercise and take a
shower?

Such questions can only be answered by the person involved
because only he knows what will revitalize him. Some people can
take a 10- or 15-minute catnap and wake up refreshed and ready to
work while others would laugh at the thought. They'd tell you that
if they went to sleep after a 10-hour to 12-hour workday, they

wouldn't wake up even if the house was on fire. Some experts say to rest up ahead of time by napping when you know your sleep will be shortchanged.

Numerous studies extol the virtues of naps. Studies by the American Academy of Sleep Medicine and the National Sleep Foundation *(www.sleepfoundation.org)* indicate that napping as few as 10 minutes can improve performance and increase self-confidence.

Research also indicates that 20- to 30-minute naps can be beneficial. A nap provides an opportunity to cool down, reenergize, and put things in perspective. (To help you fall asleep, use a face mask and/or earplugs, put on soft music, listen to an audio book, or use a favorite pillow or blanket.)

If you nap before doing important or tedious mental work, use an alarm to awaken you and have an energizing snack or drink. Arrange your environment to include bright (but nonglare) lights, cool temperatures, and upbeat music to help arouse your attention.

What about you? Think about when, where, and for how long you have napped. Think about the way the nap helped or hindered your fatigue, your ability to pay attention, and your capacity to work with concentration and accuracy.

DEMON BUSTERS: Call in the Reinforcements against the Fatigue Demon

Defend yourself against fatigue, an often unrecognized but common demon. Having a tired mind and body precludes focusing well on responsibilities at work and at home.

How can you keep away Fatigue Demons? Do these activities:

★ Adopt a healthy sleep routine.

★ Institute breaks throughout the day.

★ Monitor the effect of fatigue on your productivity and mood.

★ Review your past successes and you'll see the foundations for future action.

The **ILLNESS/MEDICATION DEMON** robs us of our vigor and can lead to emotional ups and downs. Our performance can plummet due to side effects like memory loss, confusion, insomnia, nausea, or headache.

9

Defeating the Illness/ Medication Demon

Rushing directly from a sales conference to a meeting back at home, Kate grabs the purse she took on the trip and hurries to the office. She has jet lag and her head is throbbing as her important new client drones on in a monotone. She needs to be alert but it is all she can do to maintain eye contact, smile, and take notes. Unwilling to take a break, she discretely removes her pill box from her purse and takes 2 Tylenol. As the meeting progresses, she notices that she is slurring her words and scrawling her notes. Her client asks, "Are you all right?" She assures him that she's fine, but within minutes she almost nods off! Now aware that she is definitely not all right, she excuses herself because of her headache and weaves her way to the ladies room. There she discovers that she has mistakenly taken two Ambien, a powerful, prescription sleeping aid she brought for her flight, instead of Tylenol. The slim, white tablets look and feel almost the same!

Have you ever mixed up prescriptions or taken the wrong dose of a medication like Kate?

When you're suffering from an allergy or a common cold, do you feel you're operating in a fog?

Aching muscles, dull headache, stuffy nose—your senses are numbed and your body and mind won't respond. Even the effects of the common cold can make it difficult, if not impossible, to concentrate. Common maladies such as headaches or backaches may require over-the-counter and/or prescription medications with side effects that interfere with attention, concentration, memory, sleep, and/or appetite. With more serious or chronic illnesses, the picture becomes even more complicated.

During or after an illness, mundane activities can become tiresome, even overwhelming. We may be unable to concentrate on reading or be unable to focus throughout a lengthy conversation. We may become irritated when someone asks a simple question such as "What would you like to eat?" And we may complete tasks more slowly and less accurately than when we're healthy.

This chapter examines varied ways that illness and medication can interfere with your ability to pay attention. You'll find creative ideas to help you work around these limiting factors.

Regain Focus Following an Illness

Fred loves to build things. A few days after he has surgery, he wants to keep himself busy and do a bit of building. Although he's better, he is tired, anxious, and experiencing subtle effects from the anesthesia and medications. It doesn't take long for him to notice that he's "off his building game." In the course of a morning, he misreads instructions, drops an oil can, and almost slips on the floor of the basement. During another afternoon, he cuts his finger. A few days later, he finds some hardened paint brushes that he left on the floor.

Usually a person who multitasks with ease, Fred realizes that for the time being, his inattention and distractibility prohibit doing more than one thing at a time. He decides to write out the measurements when he adjusts the size of a piece of furniture, se-lect and organize the tools and materials he will use, and plan to do less than he would ordinarily. In particular, he won't answer the phone while working because it distracts him and he's afraid of causing an accident.

Frequently, we lack the insight and awareness of the negative impact that an illness has, both physically and mentally. For example, hospital stays have been shortened from what they used to be, so patients go home earlier in their recuperation. Too often, we return to our routines without allowing sufficient time for a full recuperation from illness or surgery. Without permitting ourselves the necessary time to regain our health and strength, we prevent a full recovery and increase the likelihood of relapse or vulnerability to new illness.

The postsurgery demon can erode your performance even in your most highly skilled areas of expertise. If you've had a recent illness and you or others notice a lower level of alertness, follow these suggestions:

- Consider postponing challenges until you have fully recovered and know you can muster your attention for the time required to successfully complete the task.
- Assess your readiness to resume normal activities and discuss your situation with your physician or other healthcare provider.
- List the demands on your attention, describing when, where, what, and how well things need to be completed.
- Identify the resources and support needed to complete the task.
- Consider worst-case scenarios given the nature of your illness and the demands of the task. Then think of ways to head off those scenarios.

Possible Effects of
Medication on Performance

*Judy usually attempts to study for the real estate licensing exam
when she returns home from working in the evening. Suffering from
back pain due to a recent fall, she takes several pain medications.
Her attention wanders when she tries to study. It's all she can do to
complete her job responsibilities.*

*As her worry increases, her attention further decreases, and
she becomes more irritable both at work and at home. She thinks
she's "losing" it and will never pass the exam. Her back pain won't
let up.*

*So Judy contacts her physician and is advised to begin physi-
cal therapy. Also, she's advised to keep working but to reduce other
activities. She talks to her boss about the costs and benefits of postponing the examination for a month or two when she will be off
the medication.*

Every medication contains chemicals that may cause physical side
effects such as nausea or blurred vision.

Approximately one in six Americans suffers from chronic or
recurring pain from inflammatory disease or back pain. For example, 65 million Americans suffer from back pain while 23 million
Americans suffer from migraine headaches (at least once a year).

Many drugs used to reduce pain also affect brain function,
cause mood swings, and disturb sleep, including such drugs as
Darvon, Demerol, and Percodan (Nganele, 2004).

The National Institute of Mental Health estimates that in any
given year, nearly one adult in 10 is experiencing depression
(2006). Many adults are taking medication for this problem. Antidepressants may produce side effects that include concentration
problems, confusion, anxiety, disorientation, lack of appetite, and
insomnia. Cold/cough drugs, decongestants and antihistamines,

and bronchodilators can trigger insomnia, irritability, restlessness, and confusion.

You'll find warnings and contraindications printed on the labels of many drugs. Tranquilizers, for example, warn users to avoid taking them if they're operating machinery. Sometimes, the medication actually increases the symptoms that the medication was meant to control. That's why you should contact your healthcare provider if you notice any worsening of your symptoms and watch for side effects associated with a particular drug.

Guidelines to Minimize Side Effects of Medications

Read about medications and their possible effects (Nganele, 2004). More specifically, become more mindful of the effect a medication may have on your performance. Make a conscious effort to impose on yourself some rules and routines related to taking medications. Here are some guidelines:

What to do *before* taking a medication:

- Inform your physician of all other medicines you are taking.
- When starting on a new medication, ask your doctor, nurse, and/or pharmacist about possible side effects.
- Ask what to do if you forget to take your medication. Common sense says not to double the dose the next time you are supposed to take it.
- Establish a relationship with your local pharmacist. Use the same pharmacy for all your prescriptions so that there is a complete history of your medications and dosages.

- Read the labels, literature, and directions that accompanies the prescription.
- Throw away outdated drugs.
- Never use someone else's medication.
- Do not cut pills in half unless instructed by the physician.
- Do not mix alcohol and medication unless your healthcare provider gives permission.
- Drink four to eight ounces of water with your pill.

What to do *after* taking a medication:

- Fully close the container to prevent losing pills.
- Don't hesitate to call your doctor at the first signs of a side effect.
- If side effects occur, discuss the availability of other medications with fewer side effects.

Compliance with Medical Routines

Alfonso and Joan both develop strategies to manage their medication regimes.

Alfonso, who lives alone, has to take six medications following his surgery. He makes a chart to hang on his bathroom door. It illustrates exactly which pill or pills to take and when. This ensures that he won't take the wrong pill by mistake at night or after a nap when he is tired or inattentive. He puts an asterisk next to the pill that should be taken with food.

Since her surgery, Joan feels very confused and often loses her balance. At night, her sister counts and puts her various pills in a small cup by her bed with a bottle of water so she can take them without getting up in the middle of the night.

Just as you can have side effects from taking certain medications, you can have ill effects after taking a medication the wrong way. Some people forget to take their medications at the prescribed times. Others misread directions and take the medication at the wrong time of day or under the wrong conditions. For example, many medications should be taken after a meal while others should be taken before eating.

Unfortunately, many people are prescribed different medications by different doctors. Some combinations of drugs are contraindicated and can cause severe medical problems. The prevailing wisdom is to go to one pharmacy so there is a record of all prescribed medications. Patients are advised to check with professionals each time a new medication is prescribed. Distractibility or loss of concentration can be a sign that a medication regime is not working well.

Pay Attention to Possible Abuse

Carefully monitor your use of prescription medications. Unfortunately, there are increasing numbers of Americans abusing prescription medications, according a 2005 report by the National Center on Addiction and Substance Abuse at Columbia University.

Consider the following:

- The number of Americans abusing prescription medicine has nearly doubled in the past decade.
- More than 15 million American adults report using prescriptions for nonmedical purposes.
- Pain relievers such as OxyContin, antidepressants such as Xanax, stimulants such as Ritalin, and steroids are among the most commonly abused controlled prescriptions.

- Today, more people are abusing prescription drugs than the number who abuse cocaine, hallucinogens, inhalants, and heroin.
- Nearly 30% of emergency room deaths in 2002 related to drugs involved prescription medications, particularly painkillers.

The difficulties and distractions that occur with injuries, illness, chronic pain, and recovery may lower defenses. For any number of reasons, people can drift into a habit of taking a medication when it's no longer needed.

Because of the complexity of such problems, patients and their families are advised to work closely with their physicians and therapists to monitor the use of prescription medications.

6 Best Practices for the Effective Use of Medication

1. Use a weekly pill dispenser if several medications are to be taken at different times of the day.

2. Leave medications where you will be most likely to see them.

3. Use an alarm or signal system to remind you to take medications on time throughout the day.

4. Keep a journal or chart indicating what, when, and how much medication has been taken.

5. Note on a calendar the times when medications need to be reordered.

6. Ask your doctor, nurse, or pharmacist questions such as:

- What is the best time to take this medication?
- What should I do if I miss a dose?
- How long should I take this medication?
- Where and how should this medication be stored?

Note any medications that are addictive. Ask others to help monitor your use of these medications.

Pay Attention to Descriptions, Instructions, and Discussions

When we go to a doctor's office to discuss an operation or diagnosis, we can feel worried or fearful. Stress levels rise and attention wanes.

How many times have you left an office, called back to verify the instructions and, chagrined, learned that the information was handed to you in writing before you left the office?

Knowing that you can be vulnerable to attention glitches during such visits, try these ways to prepare to listen and pay attention:

- Bring another person (an additional pair of ears) to your appointment.
- Bring a list of questions and concerns; take notes or have someone take notes for you.
- Ask about options and worst-case scenarios.
- Ask for visual aids if you don't understand the vocabulary or procedures being discussed.
- Designate a special card case to store business cards collected from each physician or therapist.

- Get an envelope or box to store all cards, prescriptions, instructions, and billing information.
- Ask about common problems and who, where, and when to call for questions or if difficulties arise.

Steps for Dealing with Sudden Illness

At the top of her game, Marla felt that her consulting job with a Fortune 500 company was going extremely well. Then, she received a diagnosis of breast cancer. She waited for the reports that would reveal the extent and possible treatments of the cancer. Always a high achiever and stable professional, she thought that she could successfully compartmentalize her professional and private lives. She didn't think it was necessary to tell her client about her medical problem or to invite another consultant to help her.

She should have.

Although she acted cool and competent on the outside, on the inside she felt edgy and almost panicked. She awoke each morning with a nervous stomach and struggled with visualizations of herself running down the street naked, screaming that she had cancer—couldn't someone help her? In her effort to detach her business self from her all-too-human emotions, Marla uncharacteristically missed subtle communication signals from her client and failed to process the client's intended messages. The client couldn't understand Marla's seemingly insensitive behavior and decided to shelve the project Marla was hired for. She lost the contract.

One minute you are fine, the next minute, your world is turned upside down.

Whether it's an unexpected diagnosis, an accident, or sudden illness for you or a significant other, your attention gets diverted.

You have to cope with the chaos presented by life's circumstances. Certainly, being diagnosed with a serious illness interrupts business as usual.

On the one hand, it's easy to underestimate the effect of a sudden, unexpected diagnosis. But Marla's decision not to share her diagnosis with her client cost her consulting project.

On the other hand, Rosalie, a real estate agent, acted to prevent problems.

On Thursday night, Rosalie "knocked on wood" and talked about the positives in her business, family, and social life. On Friday morning, she was shopping in a boutique when her cell phone rang. As the doctor on the other end spoke, she leaned on a display case, panting and sweating, as if someone had punched her in the stomach. A diagnosis of cancer, an operation, and then, depending on the findings, who knows what. Fear and paralysis set in.

Rosalie's friend had been in a similar situation. During the next few days, her friend took on the role of Rosalie's executive assistant in charge of planning and problem solving. She helped her "catch her breath" and discuss the information, tell others, and set in motion the business-related things that had to be done before and after the operation.

Together, they developed a "to-do" list to prepare for the rounds of doctor's appointments and preoperative procedures. Rosalie needed someone to help her concentrate and organize. She knew that her brain was drained and her attention wasn't on business or anything else besides surviving the next weeks. She called her manager, hired an assistant, contacted the lawyer about her will, and located her insurance policies, and so forth.

Although she still felt like a bit of a wreck, Rosalie's actions helped her retain a certain amount of control and professionalism. By admitting that she was distracted by her illness, she averted the serious problems that can occur in the real estate business if an agent isn't always on her toes. Sacrificing working with some current clients during her treatment helped her retain her business in the long run. Being realistic and facing the challenges with support may also have helped set the stage for a speedier recovery. Luckily, Rosalie had an early stage of cancer. She came through the surgery well and within a month was getting back to her normal routine.

The advent of a sudden illness requires structure and organization so that appropriate decision making can ensue.

The following 9 steps can help to systematically deal with sudden illness:

1. Stop and deal with your emotions: cry, talk to friends and family, write in a journal, and so forth.

2. Put a temporary hold on important decisions and actions. If you must make critical decisions, get the support of a trusted friend to help you sort through the pros and cons and be your spokesperson if necessary.

3. Give yourself permission and an opportunity to rest and relax: go to the movies, take naps, listen to music, and so forth.

4. Reach out to others for support, especially those you respect who've had similar experiences.

5. Accept help, even if you think you don't need it. If you don't use the help when it's offered, ask for a rain check.

6. Take a family member or a friend to a doctor's appointment as a second pair of ears.

7. Get a notebook to record and store notes and medical records.

8. Develop a list of questions to ask.

9. Consider using self-help resources for stress, temporary sleep problems, or healing.

10 Steps to Prevent Paper Pileup

While you are ill or recovering, your mind may be unavailable to do business as usual. You may lack patience, be irritable, or be easily fatigued.

Allowing yourself time to rest and relieve yourself from the stress of feeling overwhelmed by bills, phone calls, and correspondence can help you recover more quickly.

These 10 steps to prevent the paper pileup can be applied to responsibilities at home, work, or school. Test them for yourself.

1. Give yourself permission to not deal with mail or other such chores except at special times when you are alert. Say, "I need rest. It will take twice as long, and I will make mistakes if I work without adequate attention. I have a system to avoid getting out of control."

2. Provide a reasonable time limit to your "rest from the paper pileup" and mark a possible restart day on your calendar.

3. Put mail, medication receipts, notices, and bank statements in separate folders or plastic bags. If you lack patience, throw everything in one box or plastic bag.

4. Put materials you may need to complete, mail, or other correspondence in separate boxes or plastic bags. Have a place for stamps, envelopes, return address stickers, and so forth.

5. Ask for help sorting through mail and papers. Create three piles: Urgent (e.g., bills, bank statements), Can Wait, and Possible Junk.

6. When your strength increases (or medications are decreased), allot time in 5- to 15-minute increments to get back to business.

7. Select a time when you are most alert and a comfortable place with few distractions. This may be a bed away from the desk or table you usually use.

8. Note on your calendar the number of minutes you work, even if it is only 5 minutes, and/or the number of things you accomplish (for example, 3 to 5 thank-you notes).

9. As you gain strength, add a few minutes to your work time or add a second 15-minute period of work at another time of day.

10. Congratulate yourself on a job well done.

You can protect yourself from the Illness/Medication Demon by developing a healthy lifestyle: practice healthy eating, engage in moderate exercise, get plenty of rest, schedule regular checkups, and break poor health habits such as smoking.

DEMON BUSTERS: Halt the Invasion of the Illness/Medication Demon

Be aware of the subtle but pervasive effects an illness or medication may have on your attention and/or memory. Greater awareness helps you:

★ Avoid difficulties.

★ Manage symptoms.

★ Adjust expectations.

★ Reduce stress.

★ Improve more quickly.

The **UNRULY MIND DEMON** can have three heads. It can involve a racing mind, day-dreaming, or hyper focus. The more unruly the mind, the less productive we are.

10

Defeating the Unruly Mind Demon

As a flextime public relations agent, Lois works at home two days a week. She has great powers of concentration and can work for hours on end. One day, she returns to the computer to finish writing advertising copy. She scribbles a note to remind herself to take the dinner out of the oven in 30 minutes. Sixty minutes later, her sense of smell shifts her attention from the computer to the oven, but it's too late! Facing a burned, dried-out casserole, she is aggravated with herself for not paying attention to her own note.

This is a case of hyper focus gone awry. This example illustrates but one of the elements of the Unruly Mind Demon. This demon has three heads to distract you: hyper focusing, racing thoughts, and daydreaming.

You might say that hyper focusing involves "tuning in" while daydreaming involves "tuning out." Both are essential skills with which humans have been gifted. But it's not these skills in and of themselves that can create a problem; it's their inappropriate overuse in certain situations. In terms of a racing mind, being quick-witted or fast-thinking is essential, especially during an emergency. On a daily basis, however, failure to put the brakes on "express train thinking" can create problems. The excessive use of any one or combination of these demon heads can cause you to:

• lose productivity
• not fulfill your responsibilities
• be insensitive to others' needs
• interfere with problem solving and task completion

About 20 million self-employed and wage-and-salary workers usually work at home at least once a week as part of their primary job (United States Department of Labor, Bureau of Labor Statistics, 2005). If you are one of these at-home workers, take heed.

The Unruly Mind Demon is an insidious and formidable enemy in and of itself but in combination with other demons of distraction that lurk in your home setting, you can feel that you're working all day but not getting anything accomplished.

This chapter helps you discover when and how hyper focusing, racing thoughts, and daydreaming can be problematic—and what you can do about them to keep your performance, productivity, and profit level high.

Hyper Focus

Hyper focus is intense focus, often for an extended period of time, during which you can exclude most other internal and external stimuli or interference. This type of focus usually occurs when you are doing something that is in an area of your strength and is very interesting or challenging. Sports, hobbies, and crafts are areas in which people often experience hyper focus and enjoy productivity.

Unmanaged, inappropriate hyper focus, however, can trigger problems at home and work. Here are two examples to consider.

Scenario: It is Saturday, 7:30 PM, and Jim and Janet have a plan to meet another couple. Jim is deep into the complexities of his new photo editing software.

JANET: *"Honey, it's time to get ready. The reservations are for 8:15. The last several times we went out with the Smiths, we were 20 minutes late. It's embarrassing."*

JIM: *"Mmmm yeah . . ."*

7:45 PM

JANET: *"Jim, you said to remind you to stop so you'll have time to shower, shave, and dress. Let's not be late."*

JIM: *"STOP NAGGING! Leave me alone! I'm finishing up. I know what time it is."*

Jim exemplifies a person who is hyper focused on some task or another and has difficulty stopping one activity and moving on to the next. From his point of view, his total involvement is part of his innate way of dealing with things. Once he is doing something, it is difficult for him to switch gears. From Janet's point of view such behavior is inconsiderate. It leads to family arguments and poor social relationships. Can't he try harder?

Wilma works for an insurance company. She loves details and is a hard worker. When assigned a task, she delves into it with glee. Too often, however, she gets lost in the process, developing figures and tables that aren't necessary. Even though her boss tells her "less is more," Wilma doesn't seem to get the message. She can't seem to control herself. From her boss's perspective, she wastes time,

*appears as if she doesn't listen, and interferes with the efficiency of
her department. Her job is in jeopardy.*

Jim and Wilma suffer from occasional bouts of hyper focus. They
have difficulty pacing themselves, imposing time limits, and tran-
sitioning between activities. Although often neglected in a discus-
sion of attention problems, hyper focusing can be a potential
barrier to performance. This section identifies the causes of hyper
focus and methods to better manage this tendency.

Often, the signs of hyper focusing are subtle and can be easily
ignored or defended. For example, a person who is chastised or
questioned about his or her hyper focusing might say: "I want to do
a thorough job," or "I believe that if you can't do it right, you
shouldn't do it at all," or "If you cared enough, you wouldn't make
such a big deal about it."

What's the problem with hyper focusing anyway? It's that
frequent and intense focus doesn't always lead to positive, contin-
ued performance. More often than not, hyper focusing leaves a
person dissipated and unable to complete a task with speed and
accuracy.

Activities that Involve Hyper Focus

Sometimes, we hyper focus in social situations. While interacting
with others, you may hammer a point or a question over and over
like a drill sergeant until people are rolling their eyes. You might
tell others, "This is important. Let's deal with it now." You just
can't let it go. In addition, you may be so focused on getting your
point across that you might ignore social conventions and invade
another's personal space. During such times, breaks are needed.
You need to observe the reactions of others and listen to their
feedback. You may have the focus and energy to continue talking

or working, but you need to be sensitive to the needs and preferences of those with whom you work or socialize.

At other times, you may spend excessive and unproductive amounts of time focusing on activities such as playing video or computer games, watching television, surfing the Internet, reading, talking on the telephone, listening to music or audiobooks, sports or hobbies. You may be surprised to discover that the hours have slipped away and you've missed appointments or neglected chores.

Do you have one or more activities that lead to hyper focusing that, in turn, lead to being irresponsible, unproductive, or inconsiderate?

Possible Causes of Unproductive Hyper Focus

When you hyper focus on some aspect of your job or leisure time activity, the result is likely to be positive, provided you don't get carried away. If you experience excessive hyper focus on activities that take you away from your work, life activities, or social responsibilities, then you may be creating barriers to productivity and life satisfaction.

Let's examine three common triggers for unproductive hyper focus: inadequate self-regulation of attention, fear of failure, and the perfectionism that results from confusing the pursuit of excellence with "being perfect."

1. Inadequate self-regulation.

When you inadequately self-regulate your attention, you often fail to respond to the signals that would ordinarily cause you to stop what you are doing and switch gears. You can't find the "pause" or "shift" buttons to regulate your attention. Once you start, you don't stop unless you receive some persistent interruption such as someone yelling, a phone ringing, or your body signaling exhaustion, ache, or hunger.

2. Fear of failure.

When you fear failure, you may lack effective ways of coping with your frustration or anticipation of a worst-case scenario. You try to manage the situation by controlling what you think you can control. So you sit and sit and tinker and recycle the same details over and over again. Once in this kind of cycle, you may also feel too embarrassed to reach out and ask questions or seek assistance that would improve the situation.

3. Perfectionism.

When you engage in perfectionism, you may have unrealistic standards for success. You feel that you must not stop focusing until you reach those standards, regardless of the circumstances.

For work-related tasks, you may confuse effort with excellence. You equate the dedication of more and more time and energy with a job well done. Time and energy are basic requirements of excellence but these factors alone are not a guarantee of excellence.

Excellence requires the alignment of specific tools and strategies for the completion of the task at hand. Hyper focusing may lead only to spinning your wheels. You just keep doing what you were doing, only harder and longer without the critical analysis or problem solving that might be warranted. Without taking a break or shifting gears for a while, you lose perspective and the ability to get the job done with speed, accuracy, or quality.

Research indicates that people rarely work continuously on a task without their attention and energy peaking and ebbing. Therefore, to ensure better attention, focus, and concentration, intersperse work time with break times.

Working Conditions that Contribute to Unproductive Hyper Focusing

"Take the ball and run with it." "You'll figure it out, I have confidence in you." "We'll get the specifics later." These are directions that you might receive when assigned a project at work. Too often, such directions lack clarity and specificity and you're left to your own devices to figure out what do to and how to do it. It is at such times that you may be pushed into unproductive hyper focusing; you try to find answers without adequate information or resources, only to become frustrated and waste time.

The five conditions that make us vulnerable to "focus overdrive" include:

1. Unclear goals

2. Inadequate instructions and/or shifting standards

3. Inappropriate methods or techniques

4. Insufficient feedback

5. Underestimation of the difficulty of the task or overestimation of your skill

The best defense against hyper focus in work situations is to ask for clarification and specification about tasks that are assigned. Sometimes it is necessary to be assertive, asking a variety of questions and confirming expected dates or standards.

10 Steps to Defend Yourself against Hyper Focus

Whether at work or at home, you can rely on the following steps to make you less vulnerable to hyper focus.

Here's how you can begin. Envision yourself working on a project. You're not getting much accomplished but you don't want to give up. You're not really sure how much or how well the job should be done, but since it was assigned, you feel pressure to complete it. Your uncertainty leads to stress, your lack of progress eats away at the time, and your performance begins to deteriorate rapidly. Before you get totally overwhelmed and frustrated, use the Stop, Look, and Listen technique. Say, "Stop!" Take a few deep breaths. Look what you've done and what needs to be done. Then give yourself an instruction such as "I need to switch gears to do a good job." You can also instruct yourself to reach out to others at this point for more information or assistance. By becoming aware of the early warning signals of excessive focus, you avoid putting your mind and body into overload and inadvertently bringing on a mental meltdown.

The defense against hyper focus involves creating clarity and specificity about what you need to do, how long you should engage in the activity, and how you will regulate yourself. Use some or all of the following steps to defend against unproductive hyper focus:

1. Set goals and standards before beginning a task.

2. "Guesstimate" how long the task should take and schedule ample and protected work time.

3. Write the parts or stages necessary to complete the task.

4. Estimate the time required for each step. For example, divide time for projects into stages such as brainstorming, planning, executing, and revising.

5. Make a contract with yourself to complete the tasks using the steps you outlined.

6. Set a schedule, keep track of progress using a checklist, and adjust times if necessary.

7. Program PDAs, computers, watches, and clock radios to signal times to stop activities during which you are prone to hyper focus.

8. Stop working when you know you should. For example, tell yourself to stop when the timer goes off or when you become fatigued or *antsy*.

9. Reach out to and/or collaborate with others who are skilled in the areas in which you are vulnerable.

10. Identify signals that others can provide you to help you control hyper focus. For example, request that someone call or signal you at a certain time.

It may take a bit of experimentation on your part to discover what works best for you. It did for Lois, who finally found an effective way to work and not ruin the family's dinner.

Obviously, Lois needs a different attention trigger to interrupt her writing since she so easily ignores the visual cue—her note. So she buys a kitchen timer. Twice she brings the kitchen timer to her desk and twice she turns it off to complete a few sentences, only to forget her dinner in the oven. She finally opts for setting the oven timer because its annoying noise will continue until she gets up from her chair, goes into the kitchen to turn it off, and takes her dish out of the oven.

Your Racing Mind

"I feel as if I'm on fast-forward. I'm thinking of three things at once." You can be your own worst enemy when your mind is racing. You distract yourself with thoughts that fire too rapidly.

If you are vulnerable to distractions from your racing mind, employ specific techniques to help you break the habit. These techniques sound simple but may be difficult to use consistently. For this reason, limit applying these techniques to a few important situations, tasks, or times. Two times during which a racing mind has visible negative consequences are when you engage in conversations and when you need to complete an important task.

When your mind is racing you may have a bad habit of interrupting others. You know what someone is going to say before they say it and you can't wait until the other person pauses so you can talk. This aspect of the Unruly Mind Demon has negative effects on both you and the person with whom you interact. Here are three steps to better manage that quick mind and help you listen more and interrupt less:

- Count to 10 in your mind or with your fingers (which are hidden).
- Imagine the person begging you for his or her turn to give you an important message.
- Remind yourself that there should be equal "talk time."

Joe feels as if he has a million things on his mind. At work, there's a merger. He is changing offices, responsible for training new recruits, and the team leader for three projects. At home, the kids aren't doing well in school, his mother's ill, the taxes are due, and his wife may get laid off. He's managing to balance work and life but faced with three projects and a major report, his mind is rac-

ing with all he's got to do in the near and far future. He begins to
work on his report but he has intrusive thoughts.

How often have you had a similar experience? Like a race car
driver, you need to shift gears; slow down, get into neutral, and
move on in a different, more productive direction.

If your mind is racing:

- Take a break and select a later time when you will be
  more alert and productive.
- Engage in an activity to slow down and relax. For example, stretch, take some deep breaths, write some of
  your thoughts in a journal, rest, or listen to music.
- Visualize yourself successfully completing your task.
- Imagine yourself enjoying the benefits of finishing the
  task.
- Provide yourself with instructions about how or why
  the task should be completed.
- Ward off intrusive thoughts. Say, "Stop! Now is not the
  time to think about this. Now it is time to complete this
  important task."
- Deal with bouts of untimely creativity. Make a list:
  "Great ideas that I can't act upon now." Post a sign: "I
  can't take on any more responsibilities until I finish this
  project or report."
- Pay close attention for a brief period, take a quick
  break, and resume work. Think of yourself as a sprinter
  rather than a marathon runner.
- Discuss this difficulty with your physician or mental
  health resource if a racing mind becomes a daily experience. Inability to slow your thinking may be related to a
  number of causes such as a side effect of medication, a

symptom of stress or fatigue, or a sign of Attention Deficit Disorder.

A racing mind can propel you into being overscheduled and over committed. You're on the *go, go, go*. There is always too much on your plate. You have no time to complete what you start. You don't prioritize and there is little or no time for relaxing or intimacy.

A racing mind fosters rushing and tardiness, which further robs you of energy and attention. You're always apologizing or feeling guilty and you have frequent mishaps. You may spill drinks, drop papers, forget locations, make careless mistakes, and feel overwhelmed or frustrated. The later and more frazzled you are, the less attention you can access to help you perform effectively even the most mundane tasks. Here is what happened to John.

It's the beginning of April and John, an independent CPA, is waist deep in returns. He's not good at pacing himself and is behind schedule. Files and folders are piled on the desk, floor, and chair in his home office. Faces of his clients flash before him as he runs to answer the door. The long-awaited package arrives—an attaché case for his daughter who graduates from law school in a few weeks. John has found a beautiful quality product for a great price on eBay. But while thinking of his terrific purchase, his thoughts flit from client to client and he mutters to himself about a particularly complicated return.

Eager to open the carton, John slices through the tape with a large kitchen knife. The packing tape is tightly wrapped around the box and it takes a bit of John's strength to pierce through the top. Hurriedly and haphazardly sawing through the tape, he finally opens the box enough to pull the case out. He admires the rich color and texture of the case and imagines his "princess" car-

rying it to her interviews. Then he gasps as he sees a slash across the bottom portion of the case where he pushed his knife too far into the carton.

With his mind racing and vulnerable to distraction, rushing, and impulsivity, John needs to better manage himself. He needs to stop, focus, organize, and schedule his work, not impulsively open a package. After answering the door, he might have said, "Stop. Now is not the time to open this. I need to concentrate and complete one tax return at a time."

If you experience a racing mind, assume that you will continue to waste time and effort unless you consciously try to change by employing specific strategies.

Daydreaming

Late in the day, Lana sits in a meeting that should have ended 40 minutes earlier. She's breathing in stale air while others on her team in the meeting ramble on and on. With her hands supporting her tired head, Lana's mind wanders to being on the four-day getaway cruise she recently booked.

"Lana, what do you think about the proposal?" asks the team leader.

Jarred back to reality, Lana blushes and responds, "Uh, uh, could you repeat what you said?" Lana feels embarrassed by being caught daydreaming. Inattention is not a characteristic she wants tied to her professional reputation.

Have you ever have been caught daydreaming when you should have been paying attention? Almost everyone has. Although you may feel embarrassed like Lana, you can likely escape serious negative consequences for daydreaming inappropriately. For some people, though, daydreaming negatively affects their performance and often their interpersonal interactions.

Daydreaming can help or hinder our capacity to pay attention. When daydreaming occurs at appropriate times and places, it can be beneficial. When done in excess, daydreaming interferes with our attention which in turns reduces our effectiveness on the job or in social/family situations. Better management of daydreaming, however, may yield positive results such as improved concentration, increased productivity, and greater peace of mind.

What Leads to Unwanted or Excessive Daydreaming?

Certain tasks, situations, or characteristics can set up conditions ripe for unwanted or excessive daydreaming. These include B-O-R-I-N-G tasks—those that are routine, predictable, or tedious. Not innately interesting and rewarding, they require you to give intense, conscious attention. As an alternative, daydreams provide more interesting things to think about.

Are you experiencing any of the following four conditions that can trigger unwanted daydreaming?

1. Complex or Challenging Tasks

Research reveals a great diversity within populations, with each individual having a particular profile of strengths and weaknesses. When we work in our areas of weakness, we may find the tasks tough and energy draining. As a result, we may not sustain our attention for as long as we might if we were working in our areas of strength.

Rely on these strategies to stop distraction and maintain your focus:

- Break the task into small parts.
- Identify resources that you may need.
- Make sure you understand directions for completing the task.
- Work for short but intense periods of time, taking frequent, short breaks.
- Rotate interesting tasks with the boring ones.
- Give yourself small rewards for completing each step of the task.
- Create a pleasant environment in which to complete the task.
- Get rid of an "all or none" or "now or never" attitude.

2. Unbridled Creativity

Do you know people who are extremely creative or intuitive—the ones who seem to operate in an automatic "brainstorming" mode all day long? We call these people idea generators. They love to daydream about their ideas, getting lost in the creative process, and possibly ignoring the more mundane chores of work and life.

Some people work in an innovative setting, a think tank environment. Some have a deep well of ideas and can easily come up with "out of the box" solutions. And some express themselves through poetry, art, music, or invention. Unfortunately, if you don't harness your creativity for the purpose at hand or you lapse into creative daydreaming at the wrong time, you don't act in an effective or professional manner.

The following hints can help you corral unbridled creativity and use it to your best advantage:

- Become aware of your creative thinking style and recognize if (or when) it gets in your way.
- Schedule a time and place for creative thought that allows you to fully develop your ideas.

- Keep a notebook handy and jot down spontaneous thoughts and ideas for later development.
- Understand that you'll always have more ideas than you can possibly act upon.

If your job doesn't involve enough creativity for you, perhaps you should develop hobbies or community projects that tap into your talents.

3. Stressful Situations

Faced with the need to confront or cope with uncertainty, difficulty, or stress, some people may periodically opt out of their realities by engaging in flights from reality or flights of fancy. Most people are unaware of the degree to which they use daydreaming as a coping mechanism. Procrastination may result.

You can reduce avoidance behavior by finding techniques to temporarily relieve stress and use them before beginning boring, difficult, or intense tasks. Select one or two tips from Chapter 7. For example, faced with an uninviting chore, shift from negativity to light-heartedness by using some form of humor such as reading cartoons, using a yo-yo, or listening to music or a comedian's routine.

4. Illness / Medication

Certain illnesses and/or medications can make it difficult to concentrate. At such times, people tend to turn to the inventiveness of their minds by daydreaming or just zoning out.

To minimize the side effects of illness and/or medication, review the tips offered in Chapter 9. For example, deal with your emotions when you're ill by talking to friends or writing in a journal, put a temporary hold on important decisions and actions, and give yourself permission and time to rest and relax.

If You Never Daydream, Try It

It has been said that you should hitch your wagon to a star while keeping your feet on the ground. This idea speaks to the issue of balance. While you want to avoid the negative consequences resulting from excessive daydreaming, remember that daydreaming has a variety of benefits when done at appropriate times and places.

First, daydreaming can improve your efficiency by providing time to use learning from the past to prepare for the future.

Second, daydreaming can help you to develop your creativity. When daydreaming, you can generate fanciful scenarios and consider the relationships between seemingly unrelated tasks.

Third, daydreaming can help you to regulate your emotions. Daydreaming provides an inexpensive and accessible method of relaxation. If you are periodically bored, tense, or frustrated, try taking a 3–5 minute daydreaming break. During break time you can write in a daydream journal or image an improbable but humorous story. Allow yourself to be in a restful, relaxed state when you begin to let your mind wander. Often, it is at these times that our imagination is more available.

What is Your Dream?

Those who succeed often say that their success stemmed from a dream. Their dream was an idealized or creative vision of a future condition or event. These people developed their goals as small steps leading toward their dream. Their dream helped them get ready for any opportunity that might present itself. In this regard, there is truth in the old adage, "Chance favors the prepared mind."

Although you may feel that your dream is unrealistic or unattainable, its existence helps you pay attention to your valued, and sometimes secret, desires. Give yourself the opportunity to increase your awareness and explore your secret dream(s).

Excessive hyper focusing, a racing mind, and daydreaming contribute to the confusion and chaos that exist due to any of the other demons that attack you. Be mindful of the negative effects of the Unruly Mind Demon and make a conscious effort to better manage any one of its heads.

DEMON BUSTERS: Create Countermeasures against the Unruly Mind Demon

Let the power of your mind work for you, not against you. To solve problems, make decisions and act creatively:

* Understand your strength but do not allow your strength to become a weakness.

* Structure challenging tasks in ways that will short-circuit daydreaming and channel creative impulses.

* Avoid focusing excessively on escapist activities such as video games, the Internet, or working in "overkill" mode especially when you are stressed or fatigued.

* Manage hyper focus by having clear instructions, goals, and timetables for your tasks. Use an effective attention-grabbing signal to help you end allotted work sessions.

* Practice self-calming techniques to slow a racing mind. Consult your physician if you need further support.

Be Commander in Chief:
Deploy These 10 Demon-Busting Strategies

Will you defeat or be defeated by the 8 DEMONS OF DIS-TRACTION? It's up to you.

Of course, it's difficult to give up old, ineffective habits. But that's what is needed if you want to maintain your edge in today's rapidly changing, competitive world. Even one small step can lead to spectacular results.

Plan your attack by following these 10 steps:

1. Become more mindful of how distractions interfere with your work/life performance.

2. Make a conscious commitment to avoid or reduce distractions related to tasks, settings, and yourself.

3. Identify times when you are most and least vulnerable to distraction and when you are unable to adequately access your attention reservoir.

4. Be selective. Use only the number and types of technological devices that you need.

5. Build your arsenal of defenses. Identify the strategies and tips that best meet your needs and fit your learning style.

6. Start small and set realistic goals. For example, try to reduce distractions and increase efficiency by improving upon an already existing positive situation.

7. Keep it simple. Select and adapt only one or two techniques at a time.

8. Monitor your progress and continually adjust strategies until you attain your goal.

9. Use stress management techniques, including humor, to

smooth the way and deal with the inherent ups and downs of disarming the 8 DEMONS OF DISTRACTION.

10. Reach out when things don't work out. Use your support system and/or contact special resources. World-famous performing artists, elite athletes, and top executives all have coaches and advisors. Why shouldn't you?

Mobilize for action and develop an offensive counterattack. If necessary, work with a friend or coach, but don't allow any of these 8 DEMONS OF DISTRACTION to wreak havoc with your life. Use the techniques throughout this book and enjoy your success. I did and so have countless others. You can too.

References

Alberti, R. E., and M. L. Emmons. *Your Perfect Right: Assertiveness and Equality in Your Life and Relationship,* 8th ed. Atascadero, CA: Impact Publishers, 2001.

American Society of Interior Designers. "Sound Solutions: Increasing Office Productivity through Integrated Acoustic Planning and Noise Reduction Strategies." Washington, DC: ASID, 2006.

Anderson, P. "Study: Multitasking is Counterproductive (Your Boss May Not Like This One)." CNN.com/Career, *http://archives.cnn.com/ 2001/CAREER/trends/08/05/multi tasking.study/index.html.*

Benson, H. *The Relaxation Response.* New York: Quill, 2001.

Bower, S. A., and G. H. Bower. *Asserting Yourself: A Practical Guide for Positive Change.* Cambridge, MA: Da Capo Press, 2004.

Brown, T. E. *Attention Deficit Disorder: The Unfocused Mind in Children and Adults.* New Haven, CT: Yale University Press, 2005.

Budilovsky, J., E. Adamson, and C. Flynn. *The Complete Idiot's Guide to Yoga Illustrated,* 4th ed. New York: Alpha Books, 2006.

Cardwell, D. "An Excess of Foot-in-Mouth is Linked to Lack of Shut-Eye." *New York Times,* January 7, 2004, sec. 1.

CTIA-The Wireless Association. "CTIA Public Affairs: 100 Wireless Facts." CTIA-The Wireless Association, *http://www.ctia.org/ news_media/index.cfm/AID/10257.*

Fox, K. R. "The Evidence Base for Physical Activity and Mental Health." *Public Health Nutrition,* vol. 2, no. 3a, 2004.

Greenbaum, J., and G. Markel. *Finding Your Focus: Practical Strategies for the Everyday Challenges Facing Adults with ADD.* New York: McGraw-Hill, 2005.

Hallowell, E. M., and J. D. Ratey. *Delivered from Distraction: Getting the Most out of Life with Attention Deficit Disorder.* New York: Ballantine Books, 2005.

Hayes, S. C., V. M. Follette, and M. M. Linehan. *Mindfulness and Acceptance: Expanding the Cognitive-Behavioral Tradition.* New York: Guilford Press, 2004.

Johnson, E. O. "Sleep in America: 2000—Results from the National Sleep Foundation's 2000 Omnibus Sleep Poll." National Sleep Foundation, *www.sleepfoundation.org.*

Matlen, T. *Survival Tips for Women with AD/HD: Beyond Piles, Palms, & Post-its.* Plantation, FL: Specialty Press/A.D.D. Warehouse, 2005.

McLean, L., M. Tingly, R. N. Scott, and J. Richards. "Computer Terminal Work and the Benefit of Micro Breaks." *Applied Ergonomics,* 32, June, 2001, 225 - 37.

MSN.com Money. "Shut Out From Shut-Eye; Shopzilla Survey Reveals Americans Don't Catch Enough ZZZZs." MSN.com, BusinessWire, 2006. *http://news.moneycentral.msn.com/print article.aspx?feed=BW&date=20060919&id=6032305.*

National Center on Addiction and Substance Abuse at Columbia University. Press Release: "More Than 15 Million Americans Abuse Opioids, Depressants, Stimulants; Teen Abuse Triples in 10 Years. New CASA Report: Controlled Prescription Drug Abuse at Epidemic Level." Colombia University. July 7, 2005, *http://www.casacolumbia.org/absolutenm/templates/Press Releases.aspx?articleid=397&zoneid=64.*

National Highway Transportation Safety Administration. About NHTSA: "Breakthrough Research on Real-World Driver Behavior Released: NHTSA, Virginia Tech Transportation Institute, Washington, DC: NHTSA, April 20, 2006.

National Institute of Mental Health. "Depression." Bethesda, MD: NIMH, 2001, updated September 13, 2006, *http://www.nimh.nih.gov/publicat/depression.cfm#ptdep1*

Nganele, D. *What You Must Know About Prescription Drugs: From Reducing the Cost to Avoiding Prescription Errors.* New York: JMT Print, 2004.

Patel, C. *The Complete Guide to Stress Management*. Derry, New Hampshire: Vermillion, 1996.

Rotz, R., and S. D. Wright. *Fidget to Focus: Outwit Your Boredom: Sensory Strategies for Living with ADD*. New York: iUniverse, Inc., 2005.

Seelye, K. Q. "Be Prepared; One Possible Cost of Mobile Technology: A Tired, Aching Back." *New York Times*, January 29, 2004, sec. G.

Seligman, M. E. P. *Authentic Happiness*. New York, NY: Simon and Schuster, 2002.

Solden, S. *Journeys Through ADDulthood: Discover a New Sense of Identity and Meaning with Attention Deficit Disorder*. New York: Walker & Company, 2002.

Strayer, D., Drews, F., and Johnston, W. A. "Cell Phone Users Drive 'Blind': Study Explains Why Hands-Free Phones Just as Bad as Hand-held." Salt Lake City, UT: University of Utah News and Public Relations, 2003, *http://www.utah.edu/unews /releases/03/jan/cellphone.html*.

Stress Directions: The Stress Knowledge Company. "About Stress. Personal Stress Solutions: What is Stress?" Stress Directions, *http://www.stressdirections.com/personal/about_stress/what_is_ stress.html*.

United States Department of Labor, Bureau of Labor Statistics. USDL 05-1768: "Work at Home in 2004." USDL. *http:// www.bls.gov/ news.release/homey.nr0.htm*.

Veitch, J. S., Charles, K. E., and Newsham, G. R. "Workstation Design for the Open Plan Office." *Construction Technology Update*, no 61, October, 2004.

Whitmore, J. *Business Class: Etiquette Essentials for Success at Work*. New York: St. Martin's Press, 2005.

Wyss, J. "Home is office for half of firms." The Miami Herald, September 27, 2006, *http://www.miami.com/mld/misamiherald/ 15615453 .htm?template=contentModules/printst*

Resources

Bridges, W. *Transitions: Making Sense of Life's Changes: Strategies for Coping with the Difficult, Painful, and Confusing Times in Your Life.* Cambridge, MA: Da Capo Press, 2004.

Brinkman, R., and R. Kirschner. *Dealing with People You Can't Stand: How to Bring out the Best in People at their Worst.* New York: Mc-Graw-Hill, 2002.

Chandler, S. *100 Ways to Motivate Yourself: Change Your Life Forever.* Franklin Lakes, NJ: Career Press, 2004.

Charles, C. L., and M. Donaldson. *Bless Your Stress: It Means You're Still Alive!* East Lansing, MI: Yes! Press, 2004.

Craze, R. *Teach Yourself Relaxation.* New York: McGraw-Hill, 2007.

Dahm, D., and J. Smith, eds. *Mayo Clinic Fitness for Everybody.* Rochester, MN: Mayo Foundation for Medical Education and Research, 2005.

Douglas, B. *The Idiot's Guide to T'ai Chi and QiGong.* New York, NY: Alpha Books, 2005.

Epstein, L., with S. Mardon. *The Harvard Medical School Guide to A Good Night's Sleep.* New York: McGraw-Hill, 2007.

Feigelson, S. *Energize Your Meetings With Laughter.* Alexandria, VI: Association for Supervision and Curriculum Development, 1998.

Greive, B. T. *The Blue Day Book: A Lesson in Cheering Yourself Up.* Kansas City, MO: Andrews McMeel Publishing, 2000.

————. *The Book for People Who Do Too Much.* Kansas City, MO: Andrews McMeel Publishing, 2004.

Hallowell, E. M. *CrazyBusy: Overstretched, Overbooked and About to Snap! Strategies for Coping in a World Gone ADD.* New York: Ballantine Books, 2006.

Hayes, S. C., with S. Smith. *Get Out of Your Mind and Into Your Life: The New Acceptance & Commitment Therapy.* Oakland, CA: New Harbinger Publications, 2005.

Hirshkowitz, M., and P. B. Smith. *Sleep Disorders for Dummies,* Hoboken, NJ: Wiley Publishing, 2004.

Iddon, J., and H. Williams. *The Memory Booster Workout: How to Unlock Your Mind's Potential.* San Diego, CA: Thunder Bay Press, 2003.

Knaus, W. *The Procrastination Workbook: Your Personalized Program for Breaking Free from the Patterns That Hold You Back.* Oakland, CA: New Harbinger Publications, 2002.

Leahy, R. L. *The Worry Cure: Seven Steps to Stop Worry from Stopping You.* New York: Three Rivers Press, 2006.

Lewandowski, M. J. *The Chronic Pain Care Workbook: A Self-Treatment Approach to Pain Relief Using the Behavioral Assessment of Pain Questionnaire.* Oakland, CA: New Harbinger Publications, 2006.

Lombardo, G. T. *Sleep to Save Your Life: The Complete Guide to Living Longer and Healthier Through Restorative Sleep.* New York: HarperCollins Publishers, 2005.

Luskin, F., and K. R. Pelletier. *Stress Free for Good: 10 Scientifically Proven Life Skills for Health and Happiness.* New York: HarperCollins Publishers, 2005.

Mednick, S. C., with M. Ehrman. *Take a Nap! Change Your Life: The Scientific Plan to Make You Smarter, Healthier, More Productive.* New York: Workman Publishing Company, 2006.

Pachter, B., with S. Magee. *The Power of Positive Confrontation: The Skills You Need to Know to Handle Conflicts at Work, Home, and in Life.* New York: Marlowe & Company, 2000.

Posen, D. *The Little Book of Stress Relief.* Buffalo, NY: Firefly Books, 2004.

Sarkis, S. M. *10 Simple Solutions to Adult ADD: How to Overcome Chronic Distraction and Accomplish Your Goals.* Oakland, CA: New Harbinger Publications, 2005.

Wallace, B. A. *The Attention Revolution: Unlocking the Power of the Focused Mind.* Somerville, MA: Wisdom Publications, 2006.

About the Author

Geraldine Markel, Ph.D., is an educational psychologist who is a coach, speaker, and author. She served as faculty in the School of Education, University of Michigan, and has coauthored four books on learning and performance for adolescents and adults with ADD and/or learning disabilities. These include, *Finding Your Focus: Practical Strategies for the Everyday Challenges Facing Adults with ADD, Helping Adolescents with ADHD and Learning Disabilities: Ready-to-Use Tips, Techniques, and Checklists for School Success, Peterson's Parent's Guide to the SAT and ACT: Practical Advice to Help You and Your Teen,* and *Performance Breakthroughs for Adolescents with Learning Disabilities and ADD: How to Help Students Succeed in the Regular Education Classroom.*

For more information about Managing Your Mind products (books, booklets, CDs, or digital downloads) or Managing Your Mind services (coaching and seminars), visit, *www.managingyourmind.com.* Register for a free newsletter or contact the author, *geri@managingyourmind.com*

Index

goals, focusing on, 51, 61
hyper focus, 120–127
regaining after illness,
104–105
and unruly mind demon,
119–136
Friends, 37–38
inconsiderate callers, 39–41

Goals
focusing on, 51, 61
performance goals, 27
setting, 14–15, 17, 52–53,
126, 135–137
unclear goals, 125

"Haste makes waste" syndrome,
59–62
Hyper focus
activities involving,
122–123
defending against,
123–125
designated, 120–122
unproductive hyper focus,
123–125

Illness
and daydreaming, 134
paper pileup prevention,
115–116
regaining focus after,
104–105

sudden illness, 112–115
See also illness/medication
demon
Illness/medication demon
defeating, 103–117
designated, 6, 102
Inattention
costs of, 11
and distractions, 3
plugged in, tuned out,
23–26
stress and, 78

Lockdown, electronic, 26

Managing
stress, lifestyle stress
management strategies,
84–87
technology, 32
Massage therapy, 85
Medication demon
See illness/medication demon
Medications
abuse of, 109–110
and daydreaming, 134
effective use, best practices
for, 110
effect on performance,
106–107
medical routines, compliance
with, 108–109
pay attention, 111–112

Books and Products

"No life ever grows great until it is focused, dedicated and disciplined."

—Author Unknown

mem-cards

www.mem-cards.com

Mem-Cards is a trademark of Mem-Cards Corporation

The 8 Demons of Distraction

Opportunities for distraction are everywhere, threatening to negatively affect your attention, memory, and critical thinking. Recognize the eight key "Demons of Distraction" so you can learn new habits to better manage them and reduce their effects.

Technology Demon — technology overload
Others Demon — interruptions by others
Task/Activities Demon — overscheduling, inappropriate multitasking
Places & Spaces Demon — noisy or messy spaces
Stress Demon — lapses in psychic energy
Fatigue Demon — disruptions in memory and productivity
Illness or Medication Demon — side effects of medication/recovery
8. Unruly Mind Demon — hyper focus, racing mind, and/or day dreaming

Defeating the Demons of Distraction
By Geraldine Markel, Ph.D.
©2006 Geraldine Markel, Ph.D.

NEW! Personal Coaching Card Deck:
Defeating the Demons of Distraction

This deck of 28-fast-reading, pocket-sized cards is a personal coaching tool that can be used by individuals or in corporate training. Each card contains a practical strategy and proverb to help increase work/life performance and decrease stress. In just minutes a day, you'll get everything you need to know to improve your life. Available at $9.95 each. Significant discounts available for large quantity orders from *www.managingyourmind.com*

Defeating the Demons of Distraction: 111 Ways to Improve Work/Life Performance and Decrease Stress
Geraldine Markel, Ph.D.

A handy job aid/reference, this 16-page, 3.5″×8.5″ booklet shows how to combat the competing forces that zap focus and energy at work and home. Also an ideal thank-you gift for clients, vendors, friends, and others.

$5.00 plus shipping/handling
(Inquire about large quantity discounts.)

Internet Download: $4.00

Managing Your Memory
Geraldine Markel, Ph.D.

This light and lively CD helps you discover your memory style, visualize items for better retention, minimize distractions that contribute to memory loss, and develop your memory capacity. Includes a valuable insert about how to identify your memory style, keep a memory log, and use checklists, routines, and alarms.

$12.95 plus shipping/handling
Internet Download: $10.00

Finding Your Focus: Practical Strategies for the Everyday Challenges Facing Adults with ADD
Judith Greenbaum, Ph.D. and Geraldine Markel, Ph.D.

This easy-to-use guide provides research-based techniques to help adults manage the day-to-day problems of life with ADD at home and work. The book draws upon the authors' own experience coaching people of all ages to develop workable solutions to some of the most troubling issues they face. This book offers hand-on tips to bring order to a chaotic life; learn tactics to improve memory; improve problem-solving, decision-making and goal setting skills; and manage the symptoms of ADD that hinder a satisfying life.

$16.95 plus shipping/handling

Order Form

Qty	Title	Price	Cost
	Defeating the 8 Demons of Distraction (Book) (Internet Download, $16.95)	$18.95	
	Defeating the Demons of Distraction (Card Deck)	$9.95	
	Defeating the Demons of Distraction: 111 Ways to Improve Work/Life Performance and Decrease Stress (Booklet) (Internet Download, $4.00)	$5.00	
	Managing Your Memory (CD) (Internet Download, $10.00)	$12.95	
	Finding Your Focus: Practical Strategies for the Everyday Challenges Facing Adults with ADD (Book)	$16.95	
	Subtotal		
	Sales Tax if in MI 6%		
	Shipping & Handling ($4 first book + $2 additional books)		
	TOTAL		

Please enclose check/money order (Make check payable to Managing Your Mind, LLC). Full payment must accompany order. *Visa/MasterCard accepted with online orders only.*

Mail order and payment to:
Managing Your Mind
3975 Waldenwood Dr.
Ann Arbor, MI 48105
or **order online at**
www.managingyourmind.com

Name _____

Address _____

City _____ State _____ Zip _____

Phone _____

Email _____

Downloads and large quantity discounts available at
www.managingyourmind.com